THE PALLADIO GUIDE
CAROLINE CONSTANT

D0555162

PRINCETON ARCHITECTURAL PRESS

37 East 7th Street
New York, New York 10003

© 1985, 1993 Princeton Architectural Press, Inc.
and Caroline Constant. All rights reserved.
Published 1985. Second Edition 1993.
No part of this book may be used
or reproduced in any manner without
written permission from the publisher,
except in the context of reviews.
97 96 95 94 93   5 4 3 2 1

Printed in the United States of America

Library of Congress Cataloging-in-Publication Data
Constant, Caroline.
    The Palladio guide / Caroline Constant. — 2nd ed., rev. & updated ed.
    p.   cm.
    Includes bibliographical references and index.
    ISBN 1-878271-85-7 :
    1. Dwellings—Italy—Guidebooks. 2. Architecture, Renaissance—
Italy. 3. Classicism in architecture—Italy. 4. Palladio, Andrea,
1508–1580—Criticism and interpretation.   I. Title.
NA7594.C66 1993
720'.92—dc20   93–23987
                                            CIP

Research for this book was funded in part by grants from the American Academy in Rome, the General Research Board of the University of Maryland, and the Gladys B. Delmas Foundation. I would like to thank Lucilla Marino and the staff of the Library of the American Academy in Rome for granting me access to the rare books in their collection, and Maria Vittoria Pellizzari of the Centro Internazionale di Studi di Architettura "Andrea Palladio" for her help in obtaining illustrations and permission to visit many of the buildings. I am grateful to James Ackerman, James Bodnar, Martin Kubelik, Douglas Lewis, and Cameron Roberts for their useful suggestions. I would also like to thank Douglas Oliver for printing many of the illustrations, and Alison Constant and Judith McClain-Twombly for their valuable assistance in editing the final manuscript.

CONTENTS

ANDREAS PALLADIVS VICENTINVS.

1 Andrea Palladio (Leoni, 1726)

BIOGRAPHICAL NOTE

n forty years of architectural production Andrea Palladio left perhaps the greatest legacy of any architect. Through his treatise, *I Quattro Libri dell'Architettura*, as well as by his built example, he irrevocably modified western architectural thought. During his lifetime he transformed his adopted city of Vicenza and the surrounding countryside. Despite the attention given to Palladio's work by historians in recent years, the circumstances of his life and practice remain largely conjectural *(figure 1)*.

Palladio was active in the Veneto region of northern Italy during the mid-sixteenth century, a period of unusual economic growth and cultural advancement. The political stability that resulted from Venice's control of the *terra firma*, coupled with the challenge to her domination of the seas by the League of Cambrai, prompted a shift in the region's economic base from commerce to agriculture. Land reclamation projects, resulting in an extensive canal system, facilitated this economic shift, which, in turn, prompted opportunities for architectural commissions from the rising land-based aristocracy. Because Palladio was the only notable sixteenth-century architect trained in the region, he was the first to absorb the particular economic, social, and geographic conditions of the Veneto, and incorporate them into an architecture both fundamental and innovative.

Palladio was born Andrea di Pietro in 1508, the son of a Paduan miller. Apprenticed to a stonemason at thirteen, Andrea broke his contract by 1524 and moved to Vicenza, where he joined the guild of masons and stone carvers. From 1524 to the 1540s he was associated with the Pedemuro workshop of Giacomo da Porlezza, responsible for most of the monumental, decorative sculpture in Vicenza.

It was probably around 1537 that Andrea met Giangiorgio Trissino, the Vicentine intellectual and humanist who redirected the course of his life. Trissino was rebuilding a villa at Cricoli, just outside Vicenza, where he established a learned academy to enable young aristocrats of the city to receive a classical education. According to an eighteenth-century source, Andrea was involved in the villa's renovation, undertaken by the Pedemuro workshop. Trissino took the stonemason into his academy, directed his first formal architectural education, and gave him the name Palladio.[1]

Palladio's training was unusual for the time in being specifically directed toward architecture, rather than toward more general humanist subjects. Trissino

2 *Villa Trissino, Cricoli*

was himself a humanist architect; he was responsible for the layout of his villa at Cricoli, the first building in Vicenza to evoke the classical spirit of antiquity *(figures 2, 3)*. The Villa Trissino was an important precursor to Palladio's own work. Its symmetrical layout, major central room, and loggia with flanking towers became regular components of Palladio's villas. The loggia, completed by 1538, is based on a design of Sebastiano Serlio, a variation on Raphael's Villa Madama in Rome, which Serlio published in 1540 *(figure 4)*.

Serlio was an important figure in Palladio's training, although whether this resulted from the influence of his publications or from direct contact with the theoretician himself remains unclear. Palladio may have encountered Serlio when he was in Vicenza working on the Basilica in 1539. Palladio's earliest architectural drawings, dating from this period, are indebted to Serlio's example. Serlio's five books on architecture, published individually between 1537 and 1547, comprise the first treatise to deal with architectural theory in a primarily visual, rather than verbal, manner. Palladio used illustrations from Serlio as sources for his designs, and he adopted a similar format for his own publication.

Trissino introduced Palladio to other architectural treatises available at the time. His interest in antiquity was influenced by his study of Vitruvius's first-century text, of which several sixteenth-century editions were available with interpretive illustrations. Palladio also studied Alberti's treatise and incorporated many ideas from *De Re Aedificatura* into his own *Quattro Libri* of 1570.

Between 1538 and 1540 Trissino was living in Padua. Palladio probably accompanied him during part of this period. Here Palladio's formal architectural education, begun at Cricoli, was expanded considerably. He was profoundly

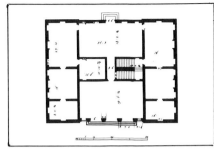

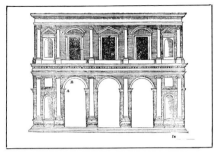

3 Villa Trissino, plan (Scamozzi, 1778)   *4 Villa Madama (Serlio, Book III, 1540)*

influenced by the Paduan humanist and architectural patron Alvise Cornaro, whose Loggia and Odeon, built in 1524 and 1530 to the design of Falconetto, were the first buildings in that city to embody the Renaissance spirit.

Cornaro's unpublished architectural treatise deals with the common dwelling — the sort of building that comprises the bulk of the city — rather than special buildings such as palaces, temples, and baths. Cornaro was interested in practical matters of economy, the logical disposition of functions, and the use of appropriate forms to convey distinction in the ordinary house. He recommended eliminating traditional orders and ornament for economic reasons and using a pediment on the domestic facade to increase a building's stature. Palladio incorporated many of Cornaro's ideas into his architecture. In addition, Cornaro's pragmatic attitude and concern with the significance of architectural form influenced the straightforward and logical verbal descriptions in the *Quattro Libri*.

Palladio's architectural career began in the late 1530s while he was associated with the Pedemuro shop in Vicenza. In 1541 Trissino accompanied him on his first trip to Rome, and Palladio's impressions of this experience were immediately apparent in his work. He returned to Rome in 1545, 1546–1547, 1549, and 1554 to study the ruins of classical antiquity, and in 1554 he published an archaeological guide to the city, *L'antichità di Roma raccolta brevemente de gli auttori antichi e moderni (The Antiquities of Rome in a Brief Compendium from Ancient and Modern Authors)*. His last journey to Rome may have been made with Daniele Barbaro, the humanist patron who commissioned Palladio to design the villa at Maser and helped him obtain many of his Venetian commissions. Between 1547 and 1556 Palladio collaborated with Barbaro to provide the architectural illustrations for Barbaro's 1556 edition of *Vitruvius (figure 5)*.

Throughout his life Palladio used his own drawings and those he copied from other architects as resources for his designs. He incorporated many of these into *I Quattro Libri dell'Architettura (figure 6)*. This important publication was intended, much as Cornaro's treatise had been, as a practical guide for the construction of useful buildings. In it Palladio elaborated building principles, using illustrations of historic buildings and numerous examples of his own work.

The four books are devoted to construction techniques and principles; private houses; public buildings and urban works; and temples. The illustrative plans and elevations of his projects often differ considerably from the executed buildings, because he idealized site irregularities and amended the designs to suit his didactic aims. The *Quattro Libri* circulated in numerous reprints and translations, with the result that for centuries Palladio's buildings were known mainly through his illustrations rather than through direct experience.

During his first decade as an architect, Palladio built palaces and country villas for the nobility of Vicenza. Giangiorgio Trissino no doubt obtained many of these commissions for his protégé as part of his campaign to modernize the city. By 1545 the esteem with which Palladio was regarded in his adopted city was indicated by the City Council's decision to entrust him with reconstruction of the Basilica, Vicenza's most important public building.

In the 1550s Palladio began to work for an expanded circle of patrons in Verona and Venice. Trissino's death in 1550 and Palladio's collaboration with Daniele Barbaro after 1549 affected this shift of patronage. During the 1560s Palladio traveled extensively in connection with his various projects. His reputation as the leading architect in Venice was established during this period, and in 1570, following Jacopo Sansovino's death, he moved to that city, where much of his late work was located. His sons Leonida and Orazio died shortly thereafter; as a memorial to them, Palladio published *I Commentari di C. Giulio Cesare (The*

5 Frontispiece, Barbaro's Vitruvius   *6 Frontispiece,* I Quattro Libri *(1570)*

Commentaries of Julius Caesar) in 1575. Palladio wrote the introductory chapter of this publication, for which his sons had executed the illustrations under his supervision.

Although Palladio's palace architecture never gained acceptance in Venice, as it had in Vicenza, a series of commissions from religious institutions, obtained through Barbaro's influence, provided him the opportunity to explore new architectural themes as well as to expand on old ones. His Venetian churches, built in outlying areas of the city, reveal the depth of Palladio's creative imagination during his final years of practice.

Palladio returned to Vicenza in 1579 to carry out his last public commission, the Teatro Olimpico. He died 19 August 1580, while working on the Tempietto Barbaro at Maser, and was buried in the Church of S. Corona in Vicenza.

[1] Palladio is an architecturally-minded angel in Trissino's epic poem, *L'Italia liberata dai Goti*; the name is borrowed from the author of an ancient agricultural treatise, Palladius.

INTRODUCTION

alladio is perhaps the most influential of western architects. Despite the familiarity of his work, it is frequently misinterpreted. The Palladian villa is often analyzed as an isolated object, unrelated to its context, and evolving toward a Neoplatonic ideal. Furthermore, his urban buildings are rarely considered in relation to the more influential rural villas. Hence the underlying spatial attitude and integral relationship to the site that his buildings share is often ignored. These views seem to arise from particularly modern sensibilities. The twentieth-century "cult of the object" and propensity for abstraction have clouded our image of Palladio, belying the visual evidence — the buildings themselves.

Rudolf Wittkower unwittingly promotes the image of the Palladian villa as a freestanding object in his well-known study of the principles of Palladio's architecture.[1] By eliminating the service wings from the villa plans to concentrate on proportional relationships within the central residential pavilions, Wittkower concludes that the evolution of the Palladian villa culminates in the Villa Rotonda *(figures 7, 8)*. Wittkower's penetrating analysis not only ignores the complexities of the villa compositions taken in their entirety, it also fails to consider several villas composed around a courtyard, with no dominant central pavilion. Subsequently, several scholars have described these examples as isolated or unusual, implying that they are inconsistent with Palladio's work as a whole.

A broader consideration of Palladio's architecture reveals an enormous variety within each category of building and the common threads running through them. Palladio's interest lay in investigating variations on architectural themes rather than progressing toward a formal ideal. He used these themes in various combinations to suit the immediate project, so that even in the formal variety of the work he maintained a consistent attitude that transcends typological distinctions.

Palladio's designs resulted from his rationalization of all aspects of the problem, particularly the site and program, as well as more general issues of significance. His attitude toward history was similarly intellectual: rather than adopt historical solutions, he created his own solutions using historical forms. Palladio's view of history was rooted in abstraction. He did not rely on formal inversions of architectural language to evolve meaning, as did many of his contemporaries, but searched instead for the essential attributes of meaning in architectural form.

Palladio's compositional methods are similarly innovative. The symmetrical juxtaposition of discrete elements about a central axis produces an effect of spatial layering that Wittkower describes as scenographic.[2] While Wittkower confines his argument to an analysis of Palladio's churches, the principles apply equally to the villas and palaces. The overall composition, no longer unified physically, is united by the logical grouping of absolute forms into a whole.[3] Palladio's spatial layering establishes a new distance between the viewer and the architectural object, one that requires the intellect to assemble the disparate elements in the mind. In this he seems closer to modern spatial sensibilities than to those of his contemporaries.

The innovative quality of Palladio's spatial vision can only be appreciated through direct experience of his buildings. Indeed, it was from the specifics of the site that a unified concept emerged, an attitude that permitted no distinction in principle between the city and the undifferentiated rural landscape. This contrasts with Palladio's method in the *Quattro Libri*, wherein he abstracted didactic principles from specific projects, removed from the exigencies of site. For centuries his projects have been known primarily as he published them rather than through direct experience. His site intentions have been obscured through the abstraction of the graphic means.

This essay traces the development of Palladio's spatial attitude as it is revealed in his drawings, villas, and urban buildings. The relationship of each building to its site is elaborated more fully in the individual building descriptions that follow.

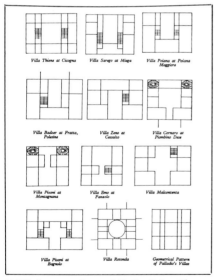

7 Wittkower, plans of Palladio's villas

8 Villa Almerico ("La Rotonda"), Vicenza

THE DRAWINGS

Palladio achieved his innovative spatial sensibility through a critical attitude toward architectural history, an attitude he applied equally to the heritage of the Renaissance as to that of classical antiquity. His drawings were the means both for Palladio's detachment from history and for his immersion in the study of its artifacts. They indicate his interest not in obtaining an historical perspective of antiquity, like the drawings of Bramante and Pirro Ligorio, but in interpreting historical artifacts in light of his own explorations into the formal and symbolic attributes of the classical language of architecture.

Many of Palladio's studies of antiquities have been preserved: some of these are adapted from drawings by other architects; many are measured drawings made during visits to various sites; others are fanciful reconstructions of ancient building complexes. Most of these drawings are rigorously frontal. Palladio seldom used perspective, except for quick study sketches, probably because it would distort the absolute value of proportional relationships; indeed, he often redrew his perspective sketches in a frontal manner *(figures 9, 10)*.[4]

The pictorial device of projecting a three-dimensional object frontally onto a two-dimensional surface created for Palladio a critical distance from the historical artifact represented. This method of abstraction allowed the drawing to be seen as an object of value in its own right, which, when reinterpreted into three dimensions, could produce results totally different from the original object. Such

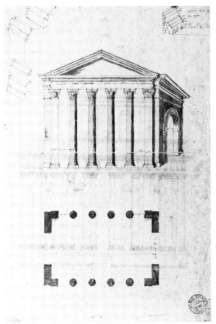
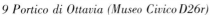
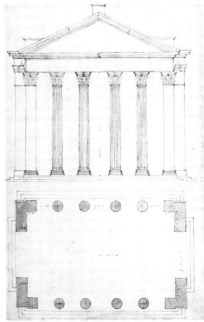

9 Portico di Ottavia (Museo Civico D26r)   *10 Portico di Ottavia (RIBA XI,18r)*

a connection exists between a Serlio plate of the villa at Poggio Reale, published in 1540, and the facade of the Palazzo Chiericati *(figures 11, 12)*. Palladio inverted three-dimensional relationships from Serlio's illustration to his facade design, so that a wall with engaged columns became an open loggia and vice versa.

Palladio's study of the Temple of Mars Ultor (RIBA XI,22r), in which he combined elevation and section with their respective orders on a single sheet, suggests the pairing of orders of different magnitudes on the Palazzo Valmarana facade *(figures 13, 14)*.[5] The giant order imparts monumental dignity to the palace, while the smaller order incorporates the scale of the adjoining buildings.

In the facade of the Redentore, Palladio extended the logic of combined orders to a spatial argument. This design is related to his drawing of the Pantheon (RIBA VIII,9r), where pedimented gables of different planes are abstracted onto a single plane. A combination of gables with corresponding orders is used to express the spatial hierarchy of the interior on a visually unified facade *(figures 15, 16)*. The objectivity gained through the drawing was Palladio's point of departure for the architectural solution; the abstraction of the drawing presaged the reinterpretation.

The distance gained through drawing allowed Palladio to use historical forms in new combinations and to derive new meanings from them. He was the first architect to systematically use the classical temple front on the private house, or at least to acknowledge the significance of that gesture. This is not because he literally believed the ancient house was so adorned, but because he wanted to enhance the stature of the private house. Palladio argued that the form of the ancient temple as the house of the gods was derived from primitive dwelling types.[6] His illustration of the House of the Ancients for Barbaro's *Vitruvius* is an example of creative interpretation rather than literal historicism *(figures 17, 18)*.

Palladio used the vaulted ceiling, a device borrowed from Roman baths, much as he used the temple portico on the facade: to elaborate the spatial hierarchy of domestic interiors *(figures 19, 20)*. He was concerned with the significance of architectural form, which lies beyond the question of symbolism in a particular cultural milieu. The creative rethinking of the logic behind architectural form provided the basis for innovation in Palladio's work, and may also account for the enduring regard for his buildings.

11 Poggio Reale (Serlio, Book III, 1540)

12 Palazzo Chiericati, Vicenza

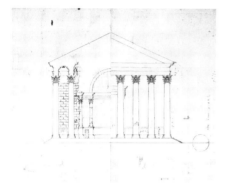

13 Temple of Mars Ultor (RIBA XI,22r)

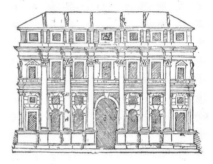

14 Palazzo Valmarana (Book II, 1570)

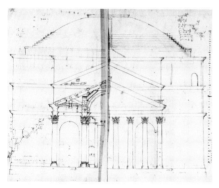

15 Pantheon (RIBA VIII,9r)

16 Il Redentore, Venice

17 House of the Ancients (Barbaro, 1556)

18 Villa Chiericati, Vancimuglio

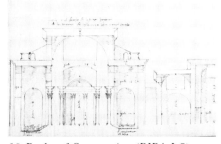

19 Baths of Constantine (RIBA I,5)

20 Villa Foscari, Malcontenta, sala

PALLADIO'S SPATIAL ATTITUDE:
THE VILLA BADOER AND THE VILLA MADAMA

Palladio's spatial attitude distinguishes his work from that of his predecessors. A comparison of Raphael's Villa Madama, which Palladio visited during one of his trips to Rome, with his own Villa Badoer at Fratta Polesine illustrates this point.

At the Villa Madama a semicircular entry court and open loggia lead through the building, first to a walled secret garden and finally to the garden itself. The villa is set laterally into its hillside site with cross-axes directed toward the view of Rome, establishing an interdependence between building and landscape. This relationship is reinforced in the entry court by the nearly equal proportions of wall to ground plane *(figure 21)*. In the bounded sequence of outdoor rooms, the building serves as a monumental gateway to the garden.

Palladio recorded his impressions of the Villa Madama in a plan drawn when

21 *Villa Madama, Rome*

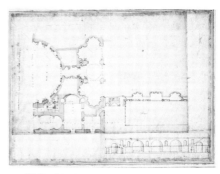

22 *Villa Madama (RIBA X,18)*

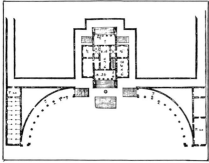

23 *Villa Badoer (Book II, 1570)*

24 *Villa Badoer, Fratta Polesine*

he visited the building in its partially completed state, much as it exists today *(figure 22)*.[7] This drawing may have influenced his plan for the Villa Badoer at Fratta, where he established an altogether different relationship to the site *(figure 23)*. Set in the flat Veneto landscape, the Villa Badoer is a bilaterally symmetrical complex, dominated by the central residential pavilion. Where the overall symmetry of the Villa Madama is modified to the conditions of the site, that of the Villa Badoer is absolute. To the modern observer the architecture does not appear to be derived from nature, as at the Villa Madama; rather, the order is of human manufacture, resulting from the logic that the mind imposes on the natural world.

At the Villa Badoer the ground is the dominant surface of the forecourt, unlike that of the Villa Madama. From the entrance, the curving wings of the *barchesse* frame the central pavilion and reach out to embrace the ground plane *(figure 24)*. The wings are low and faced with open loggias that are light and airy. In plan they are quadrants of a circle that have been pulled apart to insert the residential pavilion. The components are physically discrete; while their materials and vocabularies are related, differences in proportions and details contribute to the distinctions among them. The pavilion is pulled back from the wings and elevated on a projecting podium, so that it is separated from the adjoining elements both horizontally and vertically.

This same independence of the elements contributes to a lack of resolution in massing from any but a frontal view. The junction between the wings and the central pavilion is awkward *(figure 25)*; the rear facade is incomplete; little attention has been paid to the side elevations, where the location of each element is derived from interior considerations *(figure 26)*, unlike the entry facade, where an independent logic transcends functional accommodation.

The spatial attitude of the Villa Badoer is consistent with that in Palladio's drawings. The dominant frontality is reinforced by the rigid axial symmetry and discontinuity of vertical planes receding in depth. The wings frame the pedimented facade in a manner reminiscent of the wings and backdrop of a stage. For this reason, Wittkower calls Palladio's space conception "scenographic."

25 *Villa Badoer*

26 *Villa Badoer, view from garden*

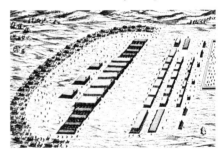

27, 28 I Commentari di Giulio Cesare

PERSPECTIVE VERSUS SCENOGRAPHIC SPACE

Scenographic space represents a break with the perspectival spatial concept of the Renaissance, as Giulio Carlo Argan has demonstrated.[8] Perspective space achieves unity through proportional relationships. It has a tangible quality; it is bounded and understood through the continuity of the wall plane. Scenographic space is physically discontinuous; its unity is perceptual rather than physical. It relies on the ground plane, rather than the wall, as datum; thus it is capable of infinite extension. The ephemeral quality of scenographic space results from the reverberations of the mind as it constructs a logical whole from the discrete components assembled on the ground plane.

Argan has linked the dissociation of perspectival space to the work of Palladio's contemporary, Michele Sanmicheli, particularly to his work on the fortifications of Verona:

> In Renaissance architecture, military architecture was a current that diverged, in which space was not an *a priori* geometric structure but simply a datum. It no longer had a constant proportional pattern but was an assemblage of objective circumstances; above all it was "ground," undulating levels, a matter of accesses and refuges, possibilities of movement and manoeuver.[9]

Palladio's interest in the spatial implications of military maneuvers is revealed in his 1575 edition of *I Commentari di C. Giulio Cesare*. Palladio supervised the execution of these illustrations by his sons, Leonida and Orazio, and the spatial strategies depicted in them are strikingly similar to his villa plans *(figures 27, 28)*.

Palladio's spatial attitude may also be traced to sixteenth-century Paduan studies in perspective, wherein perspective theory was no longer tied to optics, as it had been for Alberti, but was directed toward a general theory of relations among spectator, space, and plastic representation. Pomponius Guaricus's 1504 treatise *De Sculptura* gives priority to space rather than object; his perspective constructions are based on a horizon line rather than a vanishing point. This theoretical attitude may have influenced Palladio, whose villas present multiple horizon lines without vanishing points.

Perhaps the flat and seemingly endless quality of the Veneto landscape contributed to the novelty of Palladio's spatial vision. His most influential northern contemporaries — Michele Sanmicheli, Jacopo Sansovino, and Giulio Romano — received their early training in Florence or Rome, and their spatial ideas remained dependent on central Italian attitudes despite certain formal adaptations to northern traditions.

For Palladio the ground plane was, conceptually, a surface of human manufacture rather than part of the natural world, and hence, a *tabula rasa*. It served — much as the picture plane did for Cubism — as a base on which to conduct various experiments into the nature of three-dimensional form. By elevating the central block of the villa, Palladio stressed the idealized nature of the ground plane, creating a new ground from which to survey the surrounding domain. Without the building, we would not see the landscape in the same terms; the architecture gathers the landscape into its domain and redimensions it.

THE COURTYARD VILLAS

A building need not be the center of the composition to impose an architectural order on the landscape: a courtyard can achieve the same result. The three villas in which Palladio explored this possibility are precursors to the three-dimensional resolution of his later villas. These are usually described as lying outside his systematic approach; however, they manifest a consistent development of Palladio's spatial attitude.

Palladio's only remaining courtyard villa, at Santa Sofia, was planned for Marc'Antonio Serego after 1552 and partially executed between 1565 and 1569 (figures 29, 30). A two-story loggia of heavily rusticated columns masks a series of earlier structures, giving the villa a new coherence. The Villa Serego often is described as an anomaly in Palladio's work. Its surface articulation is unusual in his villa vocabulary, although similar rustication occurs on the back gate of the Villa Pisani, probably dating from the 1560s.

An important local influence for the Villa Serego was the nearby Villa della Torre in Fumane, built in the 1550s by an unknown architect (figure 31). Exaggerated rustication covers piers lining the major courtyard, and the rooms are composed around a sequence of open courts. The Villa della Torre must have intrigued Palladio since it resembles his plan reconstruction of the House of the Ancients (figure 32); indeed, it may have inspired his entire series of courtyard projects beginning in the 1550s, as well as the subsequent reworking of the Villa Thiene for publication in the Quattro Libri.

Palladio's second courtyard villa, built for Leonardo Mocenigo at Dolo between 1554 and 1563, was demolished in the nineteenth century. Studies for this villa progress from a central pavilion to a courtyard organization (figures 33, 34, 35, 36). In the final design the cross-axis implied within the courtyard is articulated externally in porches and gardens to either side.

A third variation on the courtyard theme was planned for the Villa Repeta at Campiglia dei Berici, designed about 1557 (figure 37). In the published version the residential quarters are suppressed volumetrically and equated with the service spaces.[10] Both functions are accommodated in one-story wings bordering a large central courtyard. The residential portion of the villa is thus subordinated to the effect of the whole. Palladio was aware of the shortcomings

29 Villa Serego, Santa Sophia

31 Villa della Torre, Fumane

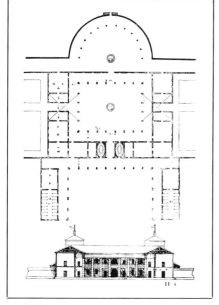

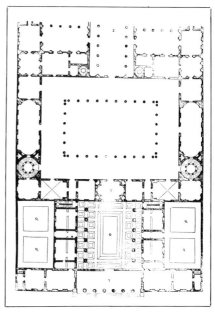

30 Villa Serego (Book II, 1570)

32 House of the Ancients (Barbaro, 1556)

and advantages of this radical approach and justified the scheme in the following terms:

> ... as the portion for the owner's residence and that for agricultural functions are of the same design, so much as the former loses in grandeur, as not being more prominent than the latter, so the whole villa gains in its ornament and dignity.[11]

By de-emphasizing the building as an object, Palladio stressed the importance of the ground plane. The sequence from entry portal to courtyard and terminal garden hemicycle of the Villa Repeta is reminiscent of the Villa Madama, rather than the House of the Ancients, and can be interpreted as an abstraction of that spatial organization. In the Villa Madama Raphael created a reciprocity between object building and object space; in the Villa Repeta Palladio gave priority to space as continuum by virtue of the dominant ground plane.

The cross-axis established in the central courtyards of these three schemes — whether implied as in Serego and Repeta or articulated three-dimensionally as in Mocenigo — is an important development over the prevailing frontality of the earlier villas. By focusing each composition on a centralized void, Palladio accentuated the ground plane and established dual frontality within the courtyard. These designs represent an intermediary step between the earlier villas — conceived frontally — and the later complexes — where dual frontality is externalized, extending control over a broader field.

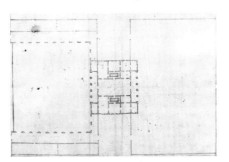

33 Villa Mocenigo study (RIBA XVI,2)

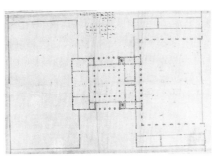

34 Villa Mocenigo study (RIBA XVI,1)

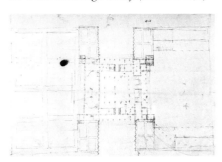

35 Villa Mocenigo study (RIBA X,1v)

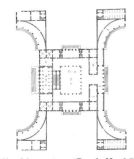

36 Villa Mocenigo (Book II, 1570)

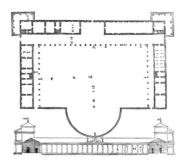

37 Villa Repeta, (Book II, 1570)

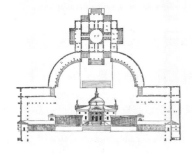

38 Villa Trissino, (Book II, 1570)

12

THE LATE VILLAS

In numerous early villas where the frontal view dominates, the side facades lack development and the garden facades are often incomplete. Palladio gradually resolved these shortcomings as the cross-axis became important to his spatial idea.

The *Quattro Libri* plan of the Villa Trissino at Meledo indicates rectilinear and curving loggias that step up the site to scenographically frame the central pavilion and establish frontality *(figure 38)*. The central block is conceived in the round, with an entry porch protecting all four faces. The porches on the major axis project from the building mass, and are thereby distinguished hierarchically from those to the sides, contained within the volume.

At the Villa Almerico — "La Rotonda" (1565/6–1569) — the cross-axis is developed to a new extreme. Unlike the Villa Trissino, the Rotonda was intended as a country residence, not a working farm; hence, without connected outbuildings, it is essentially freestanding. Though it sits atop a hillock, the villa is framed even today by cultivated hills rising beyond *(figure 39)*. The original entry was from the road below, and Palladio used the particular attributes of the site to justify his unusual rotation of the entry facade in all four directions *(figure 40)*.[12] He described the site as a theater, and, in these terms, if the hills beyond are the audience, then the villa is the sole actor in the performance. The entry axis is acknowledged on the interior by the position of the major rooms; externally, only the context differentiates the four facades.

The Villa Rotonda demonstrates that Palladio did not need garden walls or outbuildings to integrate building and site. He relied on the neighboring fields to frame the building scenographically and to establish the primacy of the entry axis. Here architecture does not dominate the site — human reason does.

39,40 Villa Almerico ("La Rotonda")

THE URBAN PALACES AND CIVIC BUILDINGS

In a passage borrowed from Alberti, Palladio reveals the urban character of his spatial attitude in his discussion about siting a villa:

> ... in the choice of the situation for building a villa, all those considerations ought to be had, which are necessary in a city house, since the city is as it were but a great house, and, on the contrary, a country house is a little city. [13]

Unlike the villas, in which he directly controlled the ground plane, on an urban site Palladio could only imply control over adjacencies. His spatial layering establishes a distance between observer and object that extends control over a broader field. In his urban buildings he relied on surface attenuation to maintain distinctions that, on a rural site, he achieved with greater economy through massing. He accomplished the effect of scenographic layering in two ways: internally, within the spatial sequence of the building, and — particularly in his mature work — externally, on the facade.

It is difficult to appreciate the full effect of the spatial sequence in Palladio's palaces, because none was completed to his intentions. Distinctions among the facade, entry hall, and courtyard are most evident in the Palazzo Thiene, where he juxtaposed independent architectural themes with common motifs to provide visual continuity. In his other palaces, thematic independence within the built segments suggests the same effect.

Palladio's second form of scenographic layering — on the surface of his

41 Palazzo Valmarana, Vicenza

42 Casa Cogollo, Vicenza

14

urban facades — is more evident in his built work. In the Palazzo Valmarana and the Casa Cogollo, which face narrow streets, Palladio compensated for perceptual restrictions imposed by the sites *(figures 41, 42)*. In the Palazzo Valmarana the giant order of pilasters dominating the central bays imparts monumental dignity to the facade; it is interwoven with a smaller order, extending the entire width, that provides continuity with the adjoining buildings. Similarly, in the Casa Cogollo the enlarged central bay interrupts the repetitive rhythm of the adjoining facades and physically extends their loggias. The compression toward the center of these two facades reinforces the entry and contributes to the scenographic effect.

Many of Palladio's urban buildings are situated on piazzas, which are transformed by his architecture. The Palazzo Chiericati, with its loggia built on public land, literally engages the space of the market and river port it originally faced *(figure 43)*. While the loggia gives the palace a rural appearance, the facade opens out to the city, reversing the spatial hierarchy characteristic of Palladio's villas. At the Redentore, where site limitations restricted the size of the piazzetta in front of the church, the facade dominates the broad Giudecca Canal *(figure 44)*.

The power of Palladio's architecture over contiguous spaces is particularly clear in the example of the Basilica. Surrounded by piazzas of different character, function, and level, the building provides a strong, unifying focus to the area through its repetitive bay system *(figure 45)*. The Basilica gathers the surrounding spaces into its purview, giving them identity.

43 Palazzo Chiericati, Vicenza

44 Il Redentore, Venice

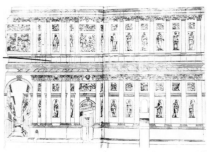

46 *Theater of the Ancients (Barbaro, 1556)*

45 *Basilica, Vicenza*

47 *Teatro Olimpico, Vicenza*

SCENOGRAPHIC SPACE AND THE TEATRO OLIMPICO

Palladio's spatial conception has been compared to the scenographic effect of traditional stage sets, the development of which originated with his contemporaries, Serlio and Scamozzi. In the Teatro Olimpico Palladio revived the antique practice of creating permanent architectural spaces for the audience and the action *(figure 46)*. These zones are distinct in treatment yet united by their juxtaposition; no proscenium arch separates them. To make this distinction Palladio relied on architectural — as opposed to painterly — means.

Palladio's studies of ancient theaters provided the inspiration for his design. The theme of his stage is derived from the triumphal arch, a device used frequently in sixteenth-century dramatic presentations. He treated the arch as a frame to a series of perspectival illusions, to be painted on interchangeable flats. Palladio most likely intended his perspectives to converge on a single vanishing point, as illustrated in his reconstruction of the ancient Roman theater for Barbaro's *Vitruvius (figure 47)*.[14] By his intended use of perspective beyond the architectural space of the stage, Palladio demonstrated that perspective is a system based on illusion rather than a representation of reality.

The traditional scenographic stage sets created by Serlio and Scamozzi were conceived in perspectival terms; this pictorial attitude was reinforced by G. B. Aleotti's introduction of the proscenium arch to separate the space of the audience from that of the action. Palladio marked the difference between these spaces by changes in architectural vocabulary alone. Furthermore, he extended the theme of architectural discontinuity to the stage itself, distinguishing the space in front of the architectural screen, constructed rationally, from that which is behind, constructed illusionistically in a foreshortened manner. The unity of the three zones derives from architectural rather than painterly principles; Palladio used scenographic means to control the entire architectural solution, not just the space of the stage.

In the history of theater design, the Teatro Olimpico was a temporary hiatus, for succeeding generations adopted the proscenium arch and painterly stage sets. Palladio's ideas are closer to the spirit of the modern theater, which favors the direct relationship of audience to action.

CONCLUSION

Palladio adopted a critical attitude toward history, rethinking the logic behind architectural form to create a new and radical type of architecture. His vision was always from within the discipline of architecture. He rejected the pictorial device of perspective to achieve visual unity in favor of the scenographic layering of space, wherein the intellect connects the diverse elements of any composition. His forms were not linked by an *a priori* system of proportions, as were those of the Renaissance; instead he sought unity through the logical grouping of absolute forms into a whole. Space was no longer preconditioned by form but generated from it.

Palladio transformed the conditions of each site, whether urban or rural, redimensioning it in a manner befitting the aspirations of the ruling aristocracy and his own architectural motivations. The power of his spatial vision can be appreciated only through direct experience of the buildings. These comments may enable Palladio's architecture to be seen afresh in the ongoing reassessment of the discipline.

NOTES

[1]Rudolf Wittkower, *Architectural Principles in the Age of Humanism* (London: Alec Tiranti, 1962), 72–73.

[2]Wittkower initiates this argument in *Architectural Principles* (97–100), and subsequently develops it in "Palladio's Influence on Venetian Religious Architecture," *Palladio and English Palladianism* (New York: Thames and Hudson, 1983), 11–15 (first published in Italian in 1963).

[3]Giulio Carlo Argan elaborates on this idea in a seminal article that departs from Wittkower's earlier conclusions: "The Importance of Sammicheli in the Formation of Palladio," in Creighton Gilbert, ed., *Renaissance Art* (New York: Harper and Row, 1970), 172–179. This article was first published in Italian in 1955.

[4]Palladio usually reserved three-dimensional drawing for his studies of details, when he used orthogonal projection to explore the volumes of particular profiles.

[5]Palladio may have seen drawings of Michelangelo's facade for the Palazzo de' Conservatori at the Campidoglio in Rome, incorporating a giant order. Michelangelo's design dates from the mid-1540s, although the facade was not executed until 1568.

[6]Andrea Palladio, *The Four Books of Architecture*, trans. by Isaac Ware, 1738 (New York: Dover, 1965), Book II, 53.

[7]In his plan of the Villa Madama (RIBA X,18), Palladio simultaneously recorded the entry spaces of the *piano nobile* with the service spaces and fishpond of the basement level. By projecting the sectional variation of the site onto a single visual plane, he effected the same spatial collapse in plan that characterizes his elevation and section drawings.

[8]Argan, "The Importance of Sammicheli," 178.

[9]*Ibid.*

[10]Because the Villa Repeta was destroyed by fire in the seventeenth century, further site research is needed to establish its fidelity to the project illustrated in the *Quattro Libri*.

[11]Palladio, *Book II*, 52.

[12]*Ibid.*, 41.

[13]*Ibid.*, 47. Alberti's phrase reads: " ... for if a City, according to the Opinion of Philosophers, be no more than a great House, and, on the other hand, a House be a little City; why may it not be said, that the Members of that House are so many little Houses.... " Leone Battista Alberti, *Ten Books on Architecture*, trans. James Leoni, ed. Joseph Rykwert (London: Alec Tiranti, 1965), 13.

[14]The perspective portion of the present stage, with diverging vanishing points, was constructed by Scamozzi on land purchased in 1580, after Palladio's death.

THE BUILDINGS

Palladio's existing buildings are arranged in chronological order. Opening hours are noted only for buildings that are officially open to visitors; admission is generally charged. THESE HOURS ARE SUBJECT TO CHANGE. Visitors should check with the Ente per il Turismo di Vicenza in Piazza Matteotti (adjacent to the Teatro Olimpico entrance) or the Centro Internazionali di Studi di Architettura "Andrea Palladio" in the Basilica for current information. The Centro is open Monday through Friday 9:30–12:15 and 3:00–5:15; Tel. 0444/ 32274–46188.

Telephone numbers are indicated for buildings that can be visited by appointment. Palace vestibules and courtyards are generally accessible on weekdays.

A NOTE CONCERNING THE QUATTRO LIBRI AND ATTRIBUTION

The lack of correspondence between a building and its illustration in the *Quattro Libri* does not mean that the project was incomplete or its design altered in construction. Palladio reworked many projects — built and unbuilt — for his 1570 publication, modifying them to the point where several published designs could never be realized on the actual sites; examples of this include the Villa Godi and the Villa Thiene (in Quinto Vicentino). Palladio's illustrations in the *Quattro Libri* are not reliable sources of information for his executed buildings, although they reveal a great deal about his architectural thought.

Nor does exclusion from the *Quattro Libri* of certain buildings completed before 1570 indicate that they are not by Palladio's hand; documentary evidence supports the attribution of many early projects, such as the Villa Gazzotti, and later additions, such as the Palazzo Schio facade, to Palladio. The reasons for such omissions are not always evident.

The publication of a project in the *Quattro Libri* may not mean that Palladio was solely responsible for its design, since preexisting structures conditioned certain projects, particularly the covered bridge in Bassano. A large number of Palladio's projects are additions and alterations, including the Basilica, the Palazzo Valmarana, and the Villa Barbaro; in many cases there is little information about these earlier structures and their influence on his designs.

BUILDING LIST

1. Villa Godi - Malinverni, Lonedo   c.1537–42, 1549–52
2. Palazzo Civena (Eretenia Nursing Home), Vicenza   1539/40–42
3. Palazzo Da Monte - Migliorini, Vicenza   1540?–45?
4. Villa Valmarana - Bressan, Vigardolo   1541–43?
5. Villa Gazzotti - Marcello, Bertesina   c.1542–47, 1550–55
6. Villa Pisani - Ferri, Bagnolo   1542–44, 1561/2–66/69
7. Palazzo Thiene (Banca Popolare), Vicenza   1542/6–58
8. Villa Saraceno - Lombardi, Finale   c.1545–48?
9. Palazzo della Ragione ("Basilica"), Vicenza   1545–80
10. Villa Thiene (Municipio), Quinto Vicentino   1545/6–1547/8
11. Palazzo Da Porto - Festa, Vicenza   c.1547/9–52
12. Villa Chiericati - Rigo, Vancimuglio   1547/8–54, 1574–84
13. Palazzo Chiericati (Museo Civico), Vicenza   1548/9–57
14. Villa Angarano - Bianchi Michiel, Angarano *(barchesse)*   1548
15. Villa Caldogno - Nordera Sacchetto, Caldogno c.1548/9–52, 1569–70
16. Villa Poiana, Poiana Maggiore   c.1549–56
17. Palazzo della Torre - Dolci, Verona   c.1549–60
18. Villa Barbaro - Luling Buschetti, Maser   c.1549/51–58
19. Villa Cornaro - Gable, Piombino Dese   1551–53
20. Villa Pisani - Placco, Montagnana   1552/3–55
21. Palazzo Antonini (Banca d'Italia), Udine   c.1552?–56
22. Villa Serego - Innocenti, Santa Sophia   1552/3?–69
23. Palazzo Valmarana - Braga, Vicenza   1554–58, 1565/6–71
24. Villa Thiene, Cicogna *(barchessa)*   1554?–56
25. Palazzo Poiana, Vicenza   c.1555?
26. Arco Bollani, Udine   1556, 1563
27. Villa Badoer, Fratta Polesine   1556/7–63
28. Palazzo Municipale, Feltre   1557–58
29. S. Maria Maggiore, Vicenza (drum and cupola) 1557–59, 1564–74

*Asterisks indicate buildings for which the attribution to Palladio is questionable.

1a Villa Godi

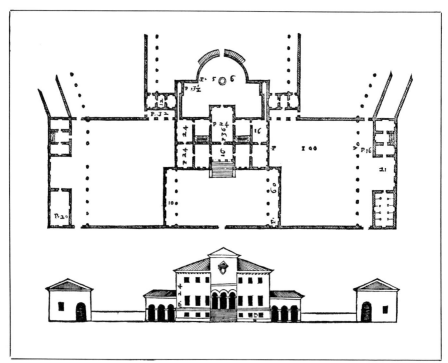

1b Plan, elevation (Book II, 1570)

1. VILLA GODI - MALINVERNI

Lonedo di Lugo (Vicenza)

Book II, plate 48   c.1537–42, 1549–52

Visit: March 15 to October 31: Tuesday, Saturday, Sunday, and holidays 2–6 (July and August 3–7). Tel. 0445/860561.

The Villa Godi is the earliest example of Palladio's independent work as an architect. Construction, well advanced before his first trip to Rome in 1541, was completed the following year. An earlier building campaign on the site resulted in construction of a *barchessa* (farm building) dated 1533. The Pedemuro workshop, with which Palladio was associated as a stonemason, may have been involved in this phase of construction.[1]

By 1540 a new building campaign began in which Palladio was specifically involved as architect. He probably incorporated an earlier residential structure; this would explain the slightly irregular angles that recur throughout the plan and the awkward relationship of the rear facade to the whole. The side wing added to the right of the main building is unrelated to Palladio's scheme. He may have been responsible for the garden layout, as the well, steps, and garden wall reflect his design. The uncompromising symmetry of the solution contrasts with the irregular site, although the building's location was probably determined by the earlier construction.

Between 1549 and 1552 Palladio revised aspects of the design in preparation for Gualtiero's fresco decorations in the right wing (1552) and Zelotti's in the central *sala* (hall) and left wing (1552–1555).

In the published plan of the Villa Godi (1570) Palladio rationalized the existing *barchessa* within a unified composition of residential and service buildings. This version is idealized and indeed could not be accommodated on the site. The villa differs substantially from the published scheme, although both rely on absolute symmetry and a hierarchical disposition of rooms around the major central *sala*.

This villa is distinguished from those of Palladio's contemporaries by its formal simplicity and restrained use of architectural ornament, which relate it directly to vernacular traditions. The design manifests the application of formal intentions to a combination of vernacular models: the open central loggia, solid side wings, and distinctive fenestration pattern (resulting from windows flanking a central fireplace in each room).

These forms are all identified with fifteenth-century Venetian palaces. However, they originally derived from a type of rural farm building, common to the Veneto, consisting of an open loggia with a single tower or flanked by twin towers. (The Ca' Brusa in Lovolo di Albettone is a well-preserved local example.) This theme of rustic origin, adapted to the urban palace in Venice, was subsequently reinterpreted by Palladio for the countryside in which it originated. The loggia's formal roots in the ancient Roman villa gave it the additional authority of an antique precedent. In the Villa Godi Palladio brilliantly combined these diverse forms to produce a new type of rural structure that is formally autonomous.

The sophistication of the entry facade reflects Palladio's primary concern for the frontal view. The garden facade is unresolved three-dimensionally, as is the junction between the central block and wings. However, in the attention to general conditions of the site and to the formal significance of the solution, this villa contains the rudiments of Palladio's architectural development.

[1]Palladio's association with the Pedemuro workshop began after he left Padua in 1524 and extended until at least 1546.

1c View of entry facade

1d Ca' Brusa, Lovolo di Albettone

2. PALAZZO CIVENA (ERETENIA NURSING HOME)

Viale Eretenio (opposite Ponte Furo), Vicenza   1539/40–42

Attribution of the Palazzo Civena to Palladio — based on drawings in the RIBA collection (XVI,11 and XVII,14) — is supported by stylistic evidence. The palace originally consisted of the five central bays of the present structure and has undergone considerable modifications in the intervening period. During renovations in 1750 Domenico Cerato changed the atrium, staircase, and garden facade. In 1820 two side wings were added by Fontana, obliterating Palladio's end facades. Finally, in 1945 the interior was completely rebuilt after damage from bombing in World War II.

The treatment of the Palazzo Civena demonstrates Palladio's awareness of contemporary architectural developments. However, it displays little of the restless surface quality of the work of his northern contemporaries, Giulio Romano in Mantua, Michele Sanmicheli in Verona, Gian

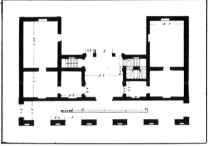

2b Plan (Scamozzi, 1776)

2a Palazzo Civena

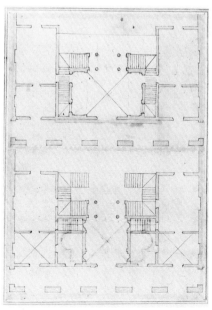

2c Plan studies (RIBA XVI,11)

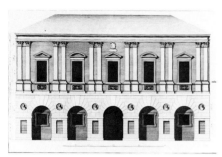

2d Elevation (Scamozzi, 1776)

Maria Falconetto in Padua, and Jacopo Sansovino in Venice. Rather, Palladio drew his inspiration from Roman architecture, particularly the work of Donato Bramante and his followers, which he would have known only from drawings.[1]

Palladio used the Venetian theme of a portico on the ground floor facing the river in a manner stylistically derived from Roman precedents. Notable features include the restrained use of rustication on the ground floor; the Serlian motif (a theme from antiquity used by Bramante in his Nymphaeum at Genazzano and published by Serlio in 1537); the combination of broad piers at the base with paired pilasters on the *piano nobile*, derived from Bramante's facade for the House of Raphael (see Palladio's drawing, RIBA XIV,11); the alternating arched and triangular tympana over the windows; and the disciplined relationship of entry portico to courtyard in plan. In these aspects Palladio used historical as well as contemporary precedents as points of departure, rethinking the logic behind architectural forms, so that the design is a carefully considered assemblage of typological motifs.

[1]Palladio first visited Rome in 1541, after the cornerstone for the Palazzo Civena was set in place.

2e Doric colonnade (Serlio, IV, 1537)

2f House of Raphael (RIBA XIV,11)

3. PALAZZO DA MONTE - MIGLIORINI
Contrada Corona, 9, Vicenza   1540?–45?

The Palazzo Da Monte is attributed to Palladio on the basis of a facade drawing in the RIBA collection (XVII,19). The facades are incomplete and hence lack compositional unity. The palace is depicted in a 1550 fresco by Fasolo, at the Villa da Porto-Colleoni in Thiene, in a form closer to the drawing than to the executed building.

The date of the project has not been established, although the building corresponds stylistically to Palladio's early investigations into the urban palace form. The inscription on the facade, "1581 Battista Da Monte," indicates a later change in ownership rather than the original construction date. The design was probably completed just before Palladio's first trip to Rome.

3a Palazzo Da Monte

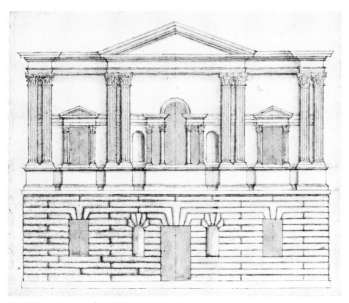

3b Elevation study (RIBA XVII,19)

4. VILLA VALMARANA - BRESSAN

Vigardolo di Monticello Conte Otto (Vicenza)   1541–43?

Ask permission to visit. Tel. 0444/596242.

This modest villa, built for Giuseppe Valmarana, is not in the *Quattro Libri*, although it essentially corresponds in plan and elevation to Palladio's drawing in the RIBA Collection (XVII,2r). This was probably the first building executed after Palladio's earliest trip to Rome; the vaulted ceilings of the smaller side rooms were influenced by his studies of Roman baths. The building was not completed as designed; the vault intended for the large entry loggia was omitted, and the attic was raised to store grain, altering the proportions of the facade.

Several farm buildings existed at the time of construction, and Palladio's building may incorporate part of an earlier structure. This would explain his use of flat, beamed ceilings in the large rooms to the rear of the house in conjunction with vaulted ceilings in the smaller rooms toward the front. Palladio's vaults are generally consistent with the spatial hierarchy of the rooms, as Alvise Cornaro suggested in his unpublished treatise; this villa is an exception to that principle.

Decorations include a beautiful frieze by Pasqualetto in the smaller central room and sixteenth-century frescoes by an unknown artist in the room to the east. The frescoes in the atrium date from the eighteenth century.

The plan resembles that of Trissino's villa at Cricoli, where Palladio worked as a stonemason and received his first formal architectural education. The inset entry loggia and hierarchical treatment of rooms, symmetrically disposed about a central axis, are comparable to the earlier building.

The gabled facade anticipates Palladio's use of the pediment — a religious theme — to elevate the significance of the rural villa, an idea he was to elaborate directly in many later buildings. The facade is incomplete; hence the *serliana* at the entry, a motif used previously in the Palazzo Civena, is not integrated into the surface as a whole. Despite the lack of resolution between the building volume and its distinct motifs, the Villa Valmarana is an interesting example of Palladio's early struggle to incorporate historical themes into an architecture both new and radical.

4a Villa Valmarana

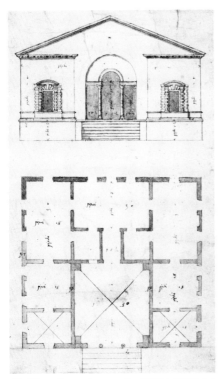

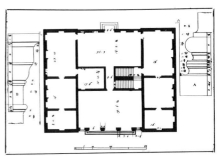

4c Villa Trissino, Cricoli (Scamozzi, 1778)

4b Elevation, plan study (RIBA XVII,2r)

29

5a Villa Gazzotti

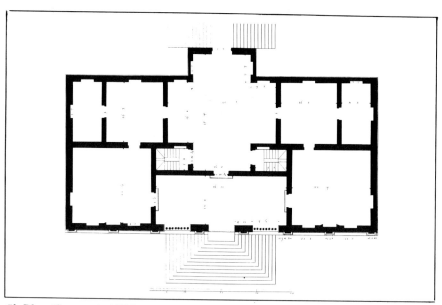

5b Plan (Scamozzi, 1776)

5. VILLA GAZZOTTI - MARCELLO
Bertesina (Vicenza) c.1542–47, 1550–55

Private; only the exterior can be seen.

Although the Villa Gazzotti is not in the *Quattro Libri*, several drawings (RIBA XVI,16A and 18; XVII,27) support the visual evidence of Palladio's hand. The building is a reduced version of the project explored in the design drawings, which includes an additional bay at either end. Built as a farmhouse for a salt tax collector, the villa consists of a linear, single-story block raised on a service basement. It incorporates an earlier structure, which is evident on the right end elevation. Palladio's design is not known to have included outbuildings; those currently on the site are of later construction.

The pediment crowning the triple-arched entry loggia imparts dignity to this modest building. The stair originally spanned the entire loggia, reinforcing the imposing character of the entry facade. This facade extends beyond the adjacent sides, and the side elevations are not composed as integral parts of the scheme, suggesting that the intention to build the end bays was suspended during construction. This is consistent with a decline in the owner's economic situation after 1545.

In 1550 Girolamo Grimani acquired the property and undertook construction of the cruciform central room. The projecting central bay is unresolved three-dimensionally, and the openings in the garden facade have since been modified.

This was the first villa to contain a cruciform central room with intersecting barrel vaults, a theme Palladio explored in the Villa Pisani at about the same time. This form developed from the T-shaped *sala* of his earlier plan drawing, which in turn derived from Venetian Gothic palaces.[1] Palladio's interior has been altered considerably. The rooms to either side of the porch originally rose the full building height to vaulted ceilings; an intermediate level has been added, with corresponding modifications to the stairs and exterior fenestration.

Despite the poor condition of this building and its considerable modifications, the Villa Gazzotti retains clear evidence of Palladio's early ability to amplify the significance of a modest farmhouse. By transposing the religious theme of a pediment to the secular domain of a rural house, Palladio elevated the triple-arched loggia, initiated in the Villa Godi, to a new level of meaning. While the overall massing is awkward, the formal resolution of the entry facade and the proportions of the cruciform central room display a masterful control of his primary architectural intentions.

[1] The Villa da Porto-Colleoni in Thiene is a noteworthy local example of a Gothic *castello* with a T-shaped *sala*.

5c View from garden

6a Villa Pisani

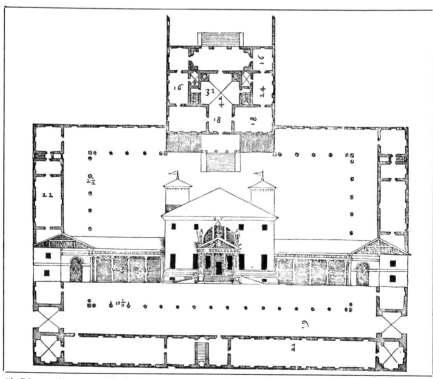

6b Plan, elevation (Book II, 1570)

6. VILLA PISANI - FERRI
Bagnolo di Lonigo (Vicenza)
Book II, plate 30   1542–44, 1561/2–66/69

Visit: Tuesday through Friday 10–12 and 2–6. Tel. 0444/831104.

Although Palladio names Vittore, Marco, and Daniele Pisani as patrons, the Villa Pisani was probably begun for their father, Giovanni Pisani, in 1542. The building originally overlooked the River Gua, which served as a major means of arrival. The integral connection to the river has been altered by the high banks raised to control flooding and the wall added in front of the villa. A 1569 drawing of the region (now in the Map Room) shows the original road leading axially toward the complex from across the river, deviating to a bridge on the left, and returning to the villa's main axis at the back gate. The integration of road network and villa organization indicates the extent of Palladio's spatial concerns.

6c Sala

The vast plantation court in an early design drawing (RIBA XVI,7) was not constructed until the 1560s. Maps of the family holdings, dated 1562 and 1569, show a large *barchessa* to the rear of the court, where there remains only a gateway of heavily rusticated piers, similar to the entry facade.[1] The surviving *barchessa* was partially rebuilt after sustaining bomb damage during World War II.

The Villa Pisani incorporates ideas from diverse sources: the semicircular entry stair was borrowed from Bramante's Cortile di Belvedere (published by Serlio in 1540), and the cruciform central *sala*, with intersecting barrel vaults, was influenced by Roman baths. The major room is distinguished spatially from those to the sides, which have flat, beamed ceilings and more modest proportions. The central *sala*, with sixteenth-century fres-

coes by an unknown artist, was originally lit from above by two large thermal windows (now altered). These appear on the incomplete courtyard facade, indicating the hierarchy of the internal organization.

The villa differs substantially from the project represented in a series of design drawings (RIBA XVII, 2v, 17, and 18r), and it is unclear why the earlier approach was abandoned. Palladio depicted the courtyard elevation rather than the entry facade in the *Quattro Libri*, perhaps indicating his dissatisfaction with the building as executed. The need to incorporate an earlier structure into the building volume may have contributed to the awkward massing of the side towers.[2] The three-dimensional articulation corresponds to Trissino's villa at Cricoli, although this could be circumstantial, owing to similar restrictions imposed by the preexisting construction.

6d View from garden

In the design of the Villa Pisani, Palladio seems to have struggled with a set of themes that could mediate between the broader spatial implications of the site and the inner spatial volumes and simul-taneously incorporate the preexisting structure. The lack of resolution in the massing may result from compromises reached during the extended period of construction. However, this is the first villa in which Palladio composed both major facades, indicating his expanding control over the primary architectural means.

With the addition of the service court in the 1560s, Palladio applied a triadic composition — first articulated clearly in the Palazzo Thiene — to the organization of this rural villa, exploiting the potential of his architecture to order a broader field.

[1]This gate resembles the unusual piers of the Villa Sarego.
[2]The earlier *castello* on the site, which included a large tower, was burned before Pisani took possession of the property.

6e Plan, elevation study (RIBA XVII,17)

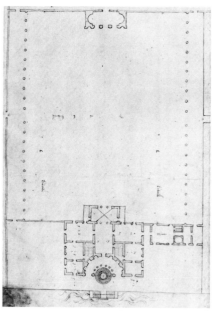

6f Plan study (RIBA XVI,7)

7. PALAZZO THIENE (BANCA POPOLARE)
Contrada Porti, 12, Vicenza
Book II, plates 8, 9, 10   1542/6–51/8

Palladio's authorship of the Palazzo Thiene is affirmed by Giorgio Vasari and by its inclusion in the *Quattro Libri*. The chronology of construction is complicated, and Scamozzi asserts that the building was begun by Giulio Romano. The robust treatment of the facades could be due either to the influence of Palladio's first trip to Rome in 1541 or to Giulio's direct participation in the early stages of the project.[1]

Construction began in 1542 and Palladio witnessed the construction contract, in which he was called stonemason rather than architect.[2] Work was soon interrupted and in 1546 the design underwent substantial revisions, apparently reflecting the improved position of the patron,

Marc'Antonio Thiene, who had also enlisted Palladio to design his villa at Quinto. The revised scheme is entirely the work of Palladio; it is his first documented investigation of the modern palace as an architectural type.

Decoration was undertaken around 1550 by Vittoria, Ridolfi, Canera, and India, all of whom contributed to Palladio's later buildings. Work was halted again in 1558 and never resumed. Thiene died in 1560.

The executed fragment of this ambitious palace corresponds to the *Quattro Libri* illustrations. Palladio may have elaborated on the actual project for his publication, as the family owned only three sides of the site. There is no indica-

7a Palazzo Thiene

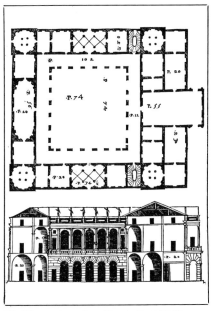

7b Plan, elevation (Book II, 1570)

7c Courtyard

tion of his intentions for the major facade toward the Corso. Furthermore, there are discrepancies between Palladio's verbal description of shops and entry loggia facing the Corso and the plan, which indicates a double layer of rooms, with the central portion projecting from the block.

The Palazzo Thiene is unlike the earlier Palazzo Civena in plan organization and surface articulation. Palladio notes in his description that this palace is "insular," referring perhaps to its antique precedents as well as its freestanding nature.[3] He borrowed the four-columned entry vestibule, an often repeated device, from Vitruvius; its form was probably inspired by the fifteenth-century oratory of San Cristoforo in Vicenza.

The overall design is more dependent on Roman Renaissance examples, particularly the work of Bramante, whom Palladio described in the *Quattro Libri* as "the first who brought good and beautiful architecture to light, which from the time

of the ancients had been hid."[4] Bramante's influence is evident in the facade articulation, the scale of the courtyard, and the additional layer of rooms toward the Corso (unexecuted), modeled after the shops of the House of Raphael.

Although the facade motifs of the Palazzo Thiene are related to Palladio's earlier palaces (particularly in the paired pilasters of the *piano nobile*), the surface articulation is new. Palladio derived this in part from the manner of Giulio Romano and also from his Roman experiences. Several drawings (RIBA XVII 6, 7, and 10B) indicate his struggle with the plastic expression of rustication on the facades and his attempt to link the high rusticated base with the more restrained *piano nobile*.[5]

The courtyard — dated 1556 and 1558 by inscriptions on its two faces — is treated independently in plan and surface. Here Palladio achieved an expression clearly his own, synthesizing the more direct influences evident on the exterior. Unlike the interior colonnades of Roman palaces, Palladio's courtyard retains the surface continuity of the wall. He differentiated between the large-scale openings of the central portion and the smaller openings of the narrow corner bays in a manner that anticipates his facade for the Palazzo Valmarana.

The Palazzo Thiene is the first of Palladio's urban buildings in which he clearly articulated a triadic composition. The facade, atrium, and courtyard are discrete zones that retain thematic independence despite their shared motifs. The individual treatment of three contiguous spaces, axially aligned, is characteristic of Palladio's work; it contributes to the scenographic quality of the spatial sequence.

7d Atrium

Whether or not Giulio Romano participated in the early stages of the project, Palladio's design for the Palazzo Thiene represents his struggle to synthesize the influence of contemporary ideas into an architecture that is both fundamental and innovative. In his later urban buildings Palladio returned to the controlled surface articulation of his earlier palaces, absorbing the mannerist tendencies of the Palazzo Thiene into a more disciplined means of expression.

[1]Giulio Romano was in Vicenza in 1542 to work on the Basilica, and he may have met with Palladio or even provided sketches for the palace.
[2]Palladio associated himself with the Pedemuro workshop until at least 1546; however, by 1540 he was recognized as an architect by Pietro Godi in connection with work on the villa at Lonedo.
[3]*Book II*, 40.
[4]*Book IV*, 97.
[5]Unlike their Roman counterparts, Vicentine palaces include living rooms on the ground floor; this alters the proportional relationships of their facades.

8a Villa Saraceno

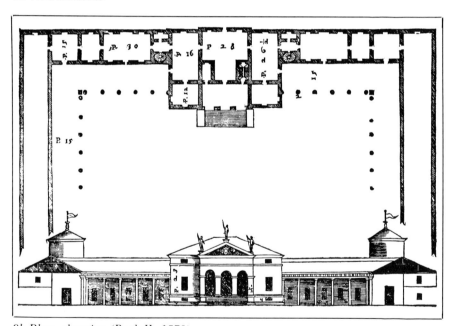

8b Plan, elevation (Book II, 1570)

8. VILLA SARACENO - LOMBARDI
Finale di Agugliaro (Vicenza)
Book II, plate 39   c.1545–48?

Private and uninhabited. The facade can be seen from the road.

Palladio designed the Villa Saraceno for Biagio Saraceno, who from 1548 held an important public office in Vicenza. Although the chronology of construction is unclear, the villa is dated on stylistic grounds as belonging to the first decade of the architect's career.

Palladio's villa was inserted within an older family complex.[1] An earlier wall and tower on the site do not appear in his illustrated plan and are not integrated into the composition. The segment of *barchessa* added to the right of the residential pavilion does not conform to the *Quattro Libri* plate, which may reflect a revised design rather than Palladio's original intentions.

The Villa Saraceno has formal and stylistic affinities with the Villa Gazzotti; each building consists of a simple linear block with a triple-arched entry loggia crowned by a pediment. Recently the entry stair has been reconstructed in concrete to match the form of the original. The barrel vault of the loggia was decorated with frescoes in the latter part of the sixteenth century. The T-shaped *sala*, with Gothic precedents, has a flat, beamed ceiling. Alterations to the central block include a partition dividing the *sala* and a small extension on the rear. The interior and garden facade are in poor condition.

Despite the ruinous state of the Villa Saraceno, it is clear that Palladio was expanding on themes initiated in the Villa Gazzotti; here the addition of the service wing increases control of the site with minimal architectural means.

[1] It stands apart from the nearby Palazzo delle Trombe, built a decade earlier by Biagio's brother, Gasparo di Giacomo Saraceno, perhaps to the design of Sanmicheli.

8c View from garden

39

9. PALAZZO DELLA RAGIONE (Basilica)
Piazza dei Signori, Vicenza
Book III, plates 19, 20   1545–80

Visit: Tuesday through Saturday 9:30–12 and 2:30–5:30; Sunday 9–12.

Two public buildings on Vicenza's main square were rebuilt between 1450 and 1460, and by 1494 they were connected by loggias. Thus unified, the Palazzo della Ragione became one of the most important buildings in the public life of the city. Its ground floor contained shops for merchants; the large hall on its upper level accommodated law courts and served as a major gathering place, much like the basilica of antiquity.

Part of the loggia collapsed in 1496, initiating a building campaign that was to continue for over a century. The City Council consulted many noted architects from the region, including Jacopo Sansovino (1538), Sebastiano Serlio (1539), Michele Sanmicheli (1541–1542), and

Giulio Romano (1542), but their suggestions were not implemented. Finally, in 1545 reconstruction of the loggia was entrusted to Palladio in association with the Pedemuro workshop. This provided him the opportunity to transform the earlier palace into a civic monument for his adopted city.

The Palazzo della Ragione was Palladio's first public commission. His appointment by the City Council indicates that by the mid 1540s the ruling nobility had confidence in his ability to provide a visual symbol of its improved status. Giangiorgio Trissino, the Vicentine humanist responsible for Palladio's architectural training, was no doubt influential in obtaining this important com-

9a Palazzo della Ragione

mission for his protégé.

In September 1545 Palladio and Trissino left for Rome, perhaps to prepare for this project. Upon his return in 1546 Palladio presented his first design to the City Council, which voted to erect a full-scale wooden mock-up of one bay on the site to judge its effectiveness. The results must have been controversial, for it was not until 1548, after another journey to Rome (1546–1547), that Palladio's revised design was approved and construction begun. The work proceeded gradually, and the loggia was only partially advanced at the time of Palladio's death in 1580. The building was completed in 1617, with decoration continuing into the mid-seventeenth century. The illustrations in

the *Quattro Libri* are idealized, in keeping with the didactic tone of the book.

This was Palladio's first building made entirely of stone, and he ranked it "among the most noble and beautiful fabricks that have been made since the ancient times."[1] His solution masks the irregularities of the underlying structure by the boldness and flexibility of its bay system, which incorporates two passageways through the center and an arcade along either end. The influence of Palladio's experience in Rome is not directly evident in the final design, which, despite its debt to Serlio's published plate of 1537, is a remarkably inventive solution.[2]

Palladio's repetitive use of the *serliana* produces a visual image of strength and solidity that is simultaneously elastic, so as to accommodate the diverse circumstances of the existing structures. It allowed him to absorb the differences in bay width by varying the side openings, and to control the proportions of height to width in each bay, while respecting the existing floor heights. By juxtaposing the *serliana*, which is visually expansive, with a trabeated system, which counter-

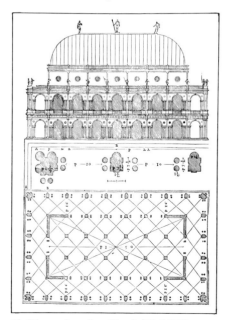

9b Plan, elevation (Book III, 1570)

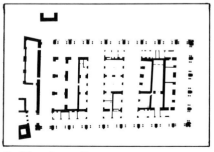

9c Plan (actual)

9d Doric colonnade (Serlio, IV, 1537)

9e Facade detail

acts those expansive tendencies, Palladio created a dynamic tension between the two systems; he reinforced this by using the same order throughout, adapted to the scale of each system.

Palladio's novel use of the Serlian motif provided the necessary flexibility to the scheme while imparting grandeur and unity to the surrounding spaces. Giulio Romano's proposal to level the adjoining piazzas and surround them with colonnades would have imposed literal unity on the area; Palladio's design relies solely on unity of the building envelope. The adjoining piazzas, which historically served different functions in the life of the city, maintain their separate identities yet are united by a visual relationship to a strong architectural center.

Although the ruling nobility of Vicenza was not always in accord concerning the design, Palladio succeeded in providing them with a symbol appropriate to their aspirations. The Basilica is to this day identified with the city, an image both eloquent and innovative.

[1]*Book III*, 76.
[2]The Serlian motif originated in antiquity; during the Renaissance it was revived by Bramante and Raphael and popularized through Serlio's 1537 publication. Palladio developed variations on the theme in a number of his well-known buildings. (See the Villa Poiana.) It became emblematic of Palladianism in England and America, where it is commonly called the Palladian motif.

10. VILLA THIENE (MUNICIPIO)
Quinto Vicentino (Vicenza)
Book II, plate 47   1545/6–1547/8

Visit: The villa is now a municipal office building and can be visited during office hours on weekday mornings 10–12:30.

Palladio's plan of the Villa Thiene in the *Quattro Libri*, depicting two houses around a central courtyard for the brothers Marc'Antonio and Adriano Thiene, has affinities to his reconstruction of the House of the Ancients. This design, unrelated to the site, represents a fanciful elaboration of the actual project, conceived for publication in 1570.

The original plan for the villa is preserved in a drawing from the collection of Inigo Jones at Worcester College. It depicts a single pavilion with flanking service wings facing the River Tesina. Only the right flank of this ambitious design was built, although considerable modifications during the intervening centuries

have obscured the relationship of the existing fragment to the original plan. The north facade facing the modern piazza corresponds to the right side of the original project; that to the south was added by Francesco Muttoni after he demolished part of the original central section of the villa, bringing about a ninety-degree shift in its primary axis of orientation. Palladio's major facades are incomplete and have been altered considerably.

Of the original interior only the barrel-vaulted corridor and four side rooms — two with frescoes by Giovanni de Mio — remain essentially as designed. It is not certain how much of the original project survived to the time of Muttoni's

10a Villa Thiene, side facade (now entry)

10b Villa Thiene, original entry facade

intervention, although *barchesse* corresponding to the original plan drawing existed in the sixteenth century.

The Worcester College plan shows Palladio's attention to the particular attributes of the site. Originally the villa faced the river, which served as the primary means of arrival. This relationship has been obscured by alterations to the building as well as by the river embankments raised to control flooding. Palladio was also responsible for the road network in the area, indicating his concern for the broader site implications.

The subtle variations between the facade to the river and that which originally faced the farm court are evident in the remaining fragments. The ambitious scale intended for this villa is also apparent in these pieces; it evokes the effect of a rural palace, befitting the status of the owner. Despite the modifications to Palladio's original facades, it is evident that the Villa Thiene represents considerable development over his earlier projects in its three-dimensional resolution as well as in its intended scope.

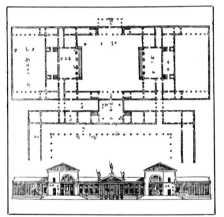
10c Plan, elevation (Book II, 1570)

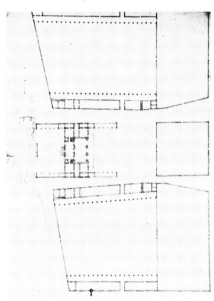
10d Plan study (Worcester College)

11. PALAZZO DA PORTO - FESTA
Contrada Porti, 21, Vicenza
Book II, plates 4, 5, 6   c.1547/9–52

The palace built for Iseppo Porto, the brother-in-law of Marc'Antonio Thiene, demonstrates the continued effort of the nobility to embellish the city with architectural symbols of its power and wealth. The date of the project is undocumented, although the initiative for its construction is assumed to have been the patron's marriage to Olivia Thiene, whose brother's magnificent palace in an adjoining street was then under construction. The plan in the *Quattro Libri* idealizes the irregular site, although we know from design drawings (RIBA XVII,9r and v) that the scope of the project was essentially as Palladio illustrated it. Only the front portion was built; the courtyard and guest house to the rear of the site were never executed.

Originally there were frescoes by Veronese on the ground floor, which were lost in the eighteenth century. Brusasorci and Ridolfi produced the frescoes and stucco decorations preserved in two rooms

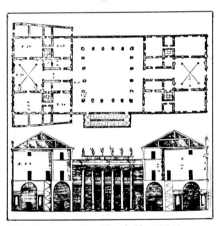

11b Plan, section (Book II, 1570)

11a Palazzo da Porto

on the ground floor. The *piano nobile* underwent devastating alterations in the nineteenth century; its present form bears little resemblance to the original layout.

The Palazzo da Porto should be compared with the earlier Palazzo Thiene, for the similarities as well as differences in these two palaces reveal a great deal about Palladio's efforts to reformulate the palace as an architectural type. His investigation into a triadic spatial organization, begun

45

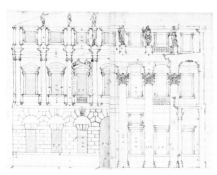

11c Elevation/courtyard (RIBA XVII,3)

11d Courtyard

in the Palazzo Thiene, is articulated more clearly in the Palazzo da Porto; however, the facade represents a return to the more disciplined manner of the earlier Palazzo Civena. This reflects Palladio's synthesis of Roman ideas as well as his increasing control over the expression of architectural elements in shallow relief. His facade stands out from the traditional Gothic palaces that line this narrow street by its bold scale and controlled, erudite surface treatment. The uncompromising relationship to the disparate angles of the adjoining palaces is an unusual affirmation of architectural individuality.

The Palazzo da Porto is similar to the Palazzo Thiene in the tripartite plan organization and independent treatment of each zone. The horizontal division of the facade corresponds to the intended breakdown in plan. Like the Palazzo Thiene, one enters through a four-columned atrium, the best preserved element of the original interior. In drawings of the unexecuted portions of the Palazzo da Porto, the central courtyard is emphasized by the scale and uniformity of its colonnade. The guest house to the rear of the court was to be smaller than the front block and to extend to the Via degli Servi. (They are identical in the *Quattro Libri* plate.)

The giant Corinthian order proposed for the courtyard colonnade contrasts with the single-story engaged Ionic columns of the facade (RIBA XVII,3, a composite of two drawings). This remarkably inventive courtyard would both separate and link the two residential blocks. It was perhaps inspired by Michelangelo's drawings for St. Peters or, more directly, by Palladio's studies of antiquity and particularly his interpretation of Vitruvius's House of the Ancients.

If the Palazzo da Porto lacks clear precedents, it is because Palladio incorporated diverse ideas — from the language of Imperial Roman architecture to the organization of the Roman Renaissance palace. In his investigations into the nature of the urban palace, Palladio never established a clear and unchanging model; rather, his ordering principles provided the basis for his explorations of diverse architectural themes.

The extraordinary proposal for the unexecuted courtyard of the Palazzo da Porto became ground for further exploration in several later projects, particularly two Veronese works, the Palazzo della Torre and the Villa Serego.

12. VILLA CHIERICATI - RIGO
Vancimuglio (Vicenza)   1547/8–54, 1574–80

Visit: April to October, by appointment. Tel. 0444/596242.

This villa was built for Giovanni Chiericati, whose brother commissioned the Palazzo Chiericati in Vicenza. Its attribution to Palladio, long contested, is now confirmed by the correspondence between his plan drawing (RIBA XVI, 20A r) and the executed building. The villa is not in the *Quattro Libri*, and, although Muttoni (1740) claimed it as Palladio's work, he did not provide plates of it.

The process of construction has been fairly well documented. Giovanni Chiericati acquired the property in 1546, when the family holdings were distributed among the three brothers. The villa was under construction by 1554, although it was unoccupied at the time of Chiericati's death in 1558. (His will indicates that roofs, dovecotes, loggias, and colonnades were yet to be completed.) In 1574 the property was purchased by Ludovico Porto, who engaged Domenico Groppino to complete construction, which continued until 1584. The present farm buildings are later additions.

The Villa Chiericati may be Palladio's first building to incorporate a freestanding entry portico. Although pedimented porticoes were used on several Renaissance villas, Palladio was the first architect to develop the theme systematically in his work.[1] He was un-

12a Villa Chiericati

doubtedly influenced by Alvise Cornaro's ideas more than by built precedents, although he may have been inspired by Tullio Lombardo's Villa Giustinian in Roncade (c. 1511–1513).

Scholars have argued that the window treatment of the Villa Chiericati is contrary to Palladio's advice in the Quattro Libri that "the windows ought to be distant from the angles or corners of the building . . . because that part ought not to be opened and weakened."[2] However, the windows correspond precisely to his plan drawing, and several other buildings by Palladio, including the Villa Godi and the Villa Zeno, have windows near the corners.

The central *sala*, a simple cubic volume with a flat, beamed ceiling, does not conform to Palladio's original design. The ambitious *sala* he proposed may have been simplified during the second phase of construction, as these changes would not have affected the foundation already in place. Palladio used the Villa Chierica-

12b View from garden

ti plan again at the Villa Foscari, without the apses of the central *sala* and with a different entry porch.

Although the impact of the Villa Chiericati was diluted considerably by the modifications to Palladio's original design, the building is significant for its entry portico, a theme that was to become emblematic of Palladianism. ism.

[1]The Villa Medici at Poggio a Caiano, built in the 1480s by Giuliano da Sangallo, is the earliest Renaissance example.
[2]*Book I*, 30.

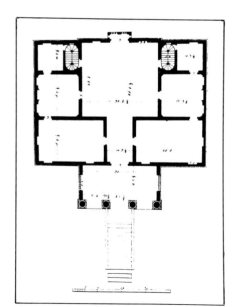

12c Plan (Scamozzi, 1796)

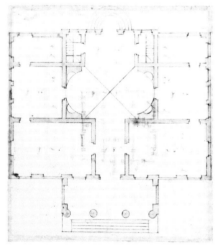

12d Plan study (RIBA XVII,20Ar)

13. PALAZZO CHIERICATI (MUSEO CIVICO)
Piazza Matteotti, Vicenza
Book II, plates 2, 3   1548/9–57

Visit: Daily (except Monday) 9:30–12 and 2:30–5; Sunday 10–12. Tel. 0444/321348.

In the Palazzo Chiericati the power of the Palladian facade to impose its order on the public space of the city is deployed literally. The patron, Girolamo Chiericati, owned a shallow piece of property on Vicenza's public market overlooking the river. In 1551, at Palladio's suggestion, he petitioned the City Council for permission to build a colonnade over the Piazza dell'Isola for his "greater comfort and the comfort and ornament of the whole city."[1] Permission was granted and the shallow dimension of the site was thus extended, so that a large *sala* could be accommodated over the colonnade built on public land. The advantage to the city equalled

that to the owner, for the significance of the public market is enhanced by the building at its edge.

Construction began immediately, indicating that the design was complete by the time the petition was put forward. By 1554, when work on the palace stopped, only the three bays of the left side and the first bay of the central portion were completed. The stucco and fresco decorations by Ridolfi and Forbicini were undertaken before 1557, when the patron died. After 1570 his son Valerio took up residence in the completed fragment. The rest of the building was executed in the seventeenth century according to Palladio's in-

13a Palazzo Chiericati

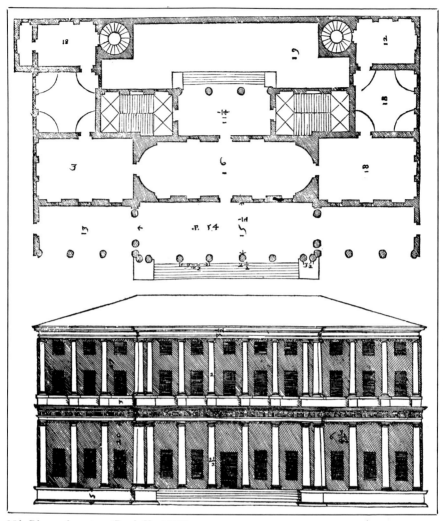

13b Plan, elevation (Book II, 1570)

tentions. The pinnacles and statues are later additions.

Palladio's studies of the public buildings of Roman antiquity no doubt inspired this unusual interpretation of an urban palace. The facade is formally related to the traditional Venetian palace loggia, although the vocabulary and massing are southern in origin. Palladio derived his design from Serlio's 1540 woodcut of the villa of Poggio Reale near Naples: he inverted three-dimensional relationships from drawing to building, so that an open colonnade became a wall with engaged columns and vice versa. The transposition of architectural themes from the public realm to the private domain and from a rural villa to an urban palace is characteristic of Palladio's radical investigation into the meanings behind architectural form.

The unusual bunching of columns in the ground-floor colonnade is a particularly inventive device to distinguish center from edge within the linear colonnade. The side facades lack formal resolution except in the portion terminating the loggia, which reinforces the frontality of the solution. Palladio's intentions for the courtyard are unknown.

The manner in which the Palazzo Chiericati dominates and gives definition to the public market resembles Palladio's villa projects. The situation of the palace — facing an open piazza on the river — seems to have prompted the open quality of the major facade, which is normally associated with a rural setting. The spatial sequence relies on increasing compression toward the center, so that the building opens outward to the piazza, reversing the spatial implications of the Palladian villa, which gathers the landscape into its domain.

The Palazzo Chiericati reveals Palladio's propensity to set aside formal precedents for an urban palace and to invent a solution based on the particular characteristics of the site as well as on the internal programmatic requirements.

13c Colonnade

[1]Lionello Puppi, *Andrea Palladio* (Boston: New York Graphic Society, 1973), 281.

14. VILLA ANGARANO - BIANCHI MICHIEL
(barchesse)

Angarano di Bassano del Grappa (Vicenza)
Book II, plate 46   1548

Private. Ask permission to visit.

Of the ambitious project illustrated in the *Quattro Libri* only the *barchesse* of the Villa Angarano were completed. These were built next to a modest farmhouse, replaced in the late seventeenth or early eighteenth century by the present residential pavilion. Palladio met with Count Giacomo Angarano at the site on three separate occasions in 1548. This was the beginning of a long and close friendship, and Palladio dedicated the first two books of the *Quattro Libri* to his patron.

The existing fragments of Palladio's project are significant for their power to structure the site. These were his first *barchesse* of this scale to be executed, although design drawings for the Villa Thiene and the Villa Poiana indicate similar intentions. The idea of integrating vast service wings into the residential nucleus of the villa was no doubt inspired by Palladio's studies of antiquity, as suggested by his fanciful reconstructions of the Forum and Sanctuary of Fortuna Primigenia at Palestrina (RIBA IX,7 and 8) — also interpreted as the Temple of Hercules Victor at Tivoli.

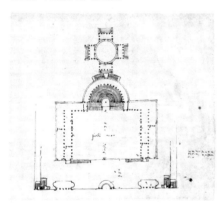

14a Sanctuary of Fortuna (RIBA IX,7)

14b Villa Angarano, barchesse

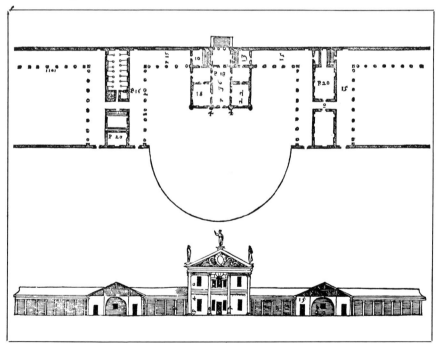

14c Plan, elevation (Book II, 1570)

15a Villa Caldogno

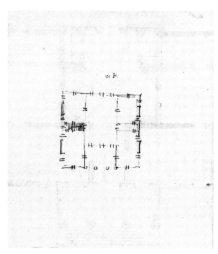

15b Plan study (RIBA XVII,20Av)

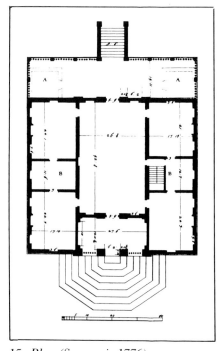

15c Plan (Scamozzi, 1776)

15. VILLA CALDOGNO - NORDERA SACCHETTO
Caldogno (Vicenza)   c. 1548/9–52, 1569–70

Visit: Summer months: Tuesday and Saturday 9–12; Thursday 3–6. Tel. 0444/585695.

Muttoni (1740) first attributed the Villa Caldogno to Palladio; his involvement is confirmed by a plan sketch in the RIBA collection (XVII, 20Av). By 1541 Losco Caldogno owned a villa at Caldogno, and he made improvements to the house in the 1540s. It is uncertain when Palladio was called in to make further modifications. He did not publish the project in the Quattro Libri, which may reflect his dissatisfaction with the final result.

In about 1569 the villa came into the possession of Losco's son Angelo Caldogno, who improved the central portion of the entry facade and inscribed his name with the date 1570.[1] He also commissioned the interior frescoes by Zelotti and Fasolo, which were completed by 1570. The fireplaces are by Lorenzo Rubini, and the statues on the gate are attributed to G. B. Bendazzoli. The external massing has been modified by the addition of two stair towers and a porch extending the full width of the building. The villa originally had no outbuildings; those currently on the site are of later construction.

Palladio regularized the plan provid-

15d Sala

15e Entry loggia

15f View from street

ing the rectangular central *sala* and smaller rooms symmetrically disposed to either side. The plan lacks the hierarchical treatment characteristic of Palladio's mature work, and the location of the stair is unresolved; this is no doubt due to restrictions imposed by the preexisting structure, which also dictated the external configuration.

The triple-arched loggia of the entry facade (now fronting a narrow drive) is similar to the Villa Saraceno. The rustication, more reserved than at the Villa Pisani, represents the sophisticated updating of an earlier idea. The motifs of the garden facade correspond with those at the entry. The oval and round windows are curious insertions below the arches, repeating those between the central *sala* and entry porch.

While the interior of the Villa Caldogno lacks the spatial elaboration of Palladio's contemporary villas, the facades display a degree of control over motifs established in earlier projects; at the same time they provided ground for experimentation.

[1] Angelo Caldogno's father-in-law was Marc'Antonio Godi, whose brothers owned the Villa Godi at Lonedo.

16. VILLA POIANA
Poiana Maggiore (Vicenza)
Book II, plate 4   c. 1549–56

Visit: Daily 9–12 and 3–6, subject to availability of custodian. Tel. 0444/898554.

Palladio was responsible for the central residential pavilion of this villa, built for Bonifazio Poiana, a Vicentine nobleman who acquired the property in 1547. The date of the project is uncertain; construction was well under way by 1555 and the decoration completed by 1563. The wing added in 1606 to the left of the central block essentially follows Palladio's published design.

The interior frescoes are by Bernardino India (grotesques) and Anselmo Canera (Emperor's Room); Bartolomeo Ridolfi was responsible for the fireplaces and stuccoes; and the statues at the entry by Girolamo Albanese were added in 1658.

Only the central portion of Palladio's scheme was realized; design drawings (RIBA XVI,4) and the *Quattro Libri* illustration reveal his interest in integrating the service elements of the Villa Poiana into a conceptual whole. The ideal nature of Palladio's proposal, as well as his refined control of the primary architectural means, distinguishes this villa from an adjoining complex owned by members of the same family.[1] In siting his villa Palladio made no reference to the earlier complex; instead, he imposed an independent

16a Villa Poiana

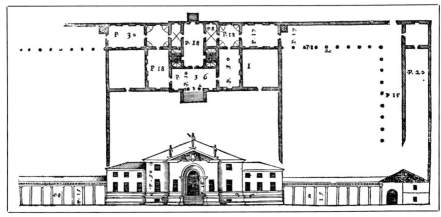

16b Plan, elevation (Book II, 1570)

order on the flat landscape of Poiana.

The entry facade includes a Serlian motif with five *oculi* in the rounded cornice, indicating Palladio's familiarity with Bramante's Nymphaeum in Genazzano.[2] Palladio's planar treatment of the *serliana* in conjunction with an inset loggia is more resolved than his earlier use of the same theme at the Villa Valmarana. At Poiana the motif is integrated

16c View from garden

spatially in the loggia and longitudinal *sala*.

The sophistication of the entry facade contrasts with the less resolved garden facade, where additional openings bring light to an intermediate level of habitable rooms. The ceiling heights of the main rooms vary in proportion to their size. This accounts for the intermediate level over the smallest rooms to either side of the central *sala*, accessible from twin stairs that lead finally to the grain storage attics above.

In the control of *chiaroscuro*, the relationship of solid to void, and the resolution of the overall massing, the Villa Poiana shows a control of the architectural means not seen in Palladio's earlier villas.

[1]The earlier Villa Poiana, across the modern road, is a typical local vernacular villa. It consists of a set of distinct elements arranged loosely around a courtyard. This arrangement reflects the gradual evolution of the complex. The tower is all that remains of a medieval *castello* on the site; a fifteenth-century loggia and later structures, including a *barchessa*, church, and residential wings, have been added to form a closed court.

[2]Palladio may have visited Bramante's rural building during a visit to Rome in 1546 or 1547. He used the *serliana* on the final version of the Basilica in a very different manner in 1548.

17. PALAZZO DELLA TORRE - DOLCI
Vicolo Cieco Padovano, Verona
Book II, plate 7   c.1549–60

Private; courtyard visible from gate. The palace is off Corso Porta Borsari near Via Quattro Spade.

Palladio designed this palace for Count Giovanni Battista della Torre, a relative of Marc'Antonio Thiene. In the published plan he greatly idealized the narrow, irregular site between the Via Quattro Spade and Via Valerio Catullo. The date of construction has not been established firmly, although by 1563 the decorations by Ridolfi and Farineti were complete. The palace remained unfinished, and after extensive bomb damage in 1945, the remaining portion of one courtyard was almost completely rebuilt.

The *Quattro Libri* plate is most likely a fanciful elaboration of the original project, the scope of which is difficult to determine. Palladio noted that "a great part" of the palace was finished.[1] At least one of the courts and part of the central loggia were realized, and they essentially correspond to the published plan and section. However, had the second courtyard been completed as Palladio illustrated, the building would extend into the Via Quattro Spade.

Site constraints prompted the unusual solution of entry from two sides into a pair of lateral courts with a central four-columned atrium. The palace was conceived without facades; Palladio's illustration depicts a section through the courts, reflecting the internalized nature of the design. The dominance of the courtyard recalls his proposal for the Palazzo da Porto in Vicenza. Palladio placed greater emphasis on vertical circulation in the Palazzo della Torre than in his earlier palaces, although the central oval stair linking the atrium with the *sala* above was

17a Palazzo della Torre

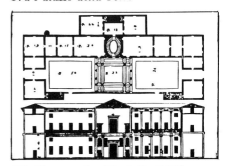

17b Plan, section (Book II, 1570)

never realized.

The role of the courtyard in the entry sequence and the discrete treatment of compositional elements suggest that Palladio conceived of the Palazzo della Torre as a microcosm of the urban situation.

[1]*Book II*, 40.

18a Villa Barbaro

18b Original approach

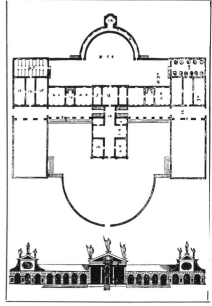

18c Plan, elevation (Book II, 1570)

18. VILLA BARBARO - LULING BUSCHETTI

Maser (Treviso)

Book II, plate 34   c.1549/51–58

Visit: March to October: Tuesday, Saturday, Sunday 3–6; (November to February: 2:30–5). On Tuesdays the Tempietto interior can be seen by request. Tel. 0423/565002.

The Villa Barbaro was built for the distinguished humanists Daniele and Marc' Antonio Barbaro. The project was probably begun in 1549, and construction was well advanced by 1558.

The brothers were architectural experts. Daniele Barbaro was a papal prelate and the author of an annotated edition of *Vitruvius* (1556), for which Palladio provided the architectural illustrations. Their collaboration began in 1549, and Barbaro may have accompanied Palladio to Rome in 1554. Marc'Antonio Barbaro was an influential Venetian statesman who was active in the public building projects of that city from 1574 until his death in 1595; he designed and executed much of the villa's sculptural decoration. The intervention of both patrons in the villa's conception and execution may account for its eclectic quality, which is without precedent in Palladio's work.

The Villa Barbaro is built on the remains of a medieval *castello* at the edge of the Dolomite foothills. The earlier walls survive to the height of the projecting residential block, and in the attic there are remains of medieval fireplaces. The lateral wings correspond to the earlier moat: they extend in a linear fashion, separating the wooded hillside from the flat arable fields below. The original entry was through the agricultural fields along the main axis of the villa. (The present road is more recent.)

The villa was a rural retreat as well as a working farm. The wings framing the central residential pavilion may reflect a local vernacular tradition, for the pre-Palladian villa at Cusignana di Arcade also has outstretched service wings, as does Palladio's second villa in Treviso, the Villa Emo. At Maser the wings end in dovecotes; these are more scenographic than pragmatic, however, as the working *barchesse* are set apart, out of view of the residential complex.

The Villa Barbaro has qualities not usually associated with Palladio's work. The central axis ends in a hemicycle set into the hill, articulated as a *nymphaeum*. The main living floor is raised a full story above the ground to be level with the *nymphaeum* and to afford a magnificent view of the family's extensive agricultural holdings. Four Ionic columns adapted from the Temple of Fortuna Virilis in Rome adorn the projecting residential block. The entry stairs are concealed within the central volume at the junction of the lateral wings. (Palladio's earlier design incorporating a large central staircase was abandoned as impractical.)

The *nymphaeum* is the critical element of the sectional idea, and, because it is unique to Palladio's work, it may have been conceived by the patrons. They were no doubt influenced by contemporary Roman villas, which emulated those from antiquity described by Pliny and Vitruvius. Vignola's *nymphaeum* for the Villa Giulia (built between 1551 and 1553) and Pirro Ligorio's plans for the Villa d'Este at Tivoli were possible precedents.[1] The inspiration of the antique is explicit in a fresco by Veronese (in the small central

18d Fireplace

room adjacent to the *nymphaeum*), in which the Villa Barbaro is depicted in a landscape of ancient buildings.

The villa's decorative scheme is part of an iconographic program conceived by the patrons, who supervised much of its extended execution. Daniele and Marc' Antonio Barbaro probably solicited Veronese to provide the fresco decorations, executed between 1560 and 1562, since Palladio does not mention the painter's involvement in the *Quattro Libri*. Veronese's pictorial layering corresponds in many ways to Palladio's spatial attitude, with the result that the frescoes amplify the architecture. Indeed, a more fitting marriage of architecture and painting is difficult to imagine. The sculptural decoration may be entirely the work of Marc' Antonio Barbaro; the fireplaces are particularly noteworthy.

The transposition of architectural themes from various sources was common in Palladio's work, although he usually abstracted the ideas rather than explicitly rendering a model. At the Villa Barbaro this level of abstraction is missing: the architecture and its decoration are explicitly referential. Palladio attempted to assimilate his patrons' intentions within an overall architectural idea by abstracting the natural conditions of the site in the extended wings and *nymphaeum* as well as through the villa's strong physical presence. In seeking to transform the conditions of the site, to redimension it, the villa celebrates the ideology of rural, agricultural life.

[1]Palladio met Ligorio in 1554, and they probably discussed his unexecuted plans for the Tivoli villa at that time.

18e Nymphaeum

19. VILLA CORNARO - GABLE

Piombino Dese (Padova)

Book II, plate 36   1551–53

Visit: May through October: Saturday 3:30–6; year-round to groups of ten or more by appointment with custodian, Signor Miolo. Tel. 049/9365017.

Giorgio Cornaro inherited a portion of his family's property in Piombino Dese upon the death of his father in 1551. He immediately engaged Palladio to design a villa, and construction began the next year. The house was inhabited by 1554 yet remained unfinished until about 1590, when the side wings were added following Palladio's published design.

The villa has been restored carefully and retains many of its original materials, including brick tile and terrazzo floors, oval stairs, and elements of the garden loggia. The atrium statues of Cornaro family members are attributed to Camillo Mariano (c.1596). The interior frescoes by Mattia Bartolani and stucco work by

Cabianca date from the eighteenth century.

The two major living floors give the villa an urban character appropriate to its location on the town's main street. The overall form parallels the Villa Pisani in Montagnana and the Palazzo Antonini in Udine of the same period; all are variations on the theme of palace-villa.

At the Villa Cornaro a projecting two-story loggia surmounted by a classical pediment marks the major entry, while that facing the garden is recessed. This form of loggia derives from the traditional Venetian palace facade, although the motif originated in rustic farm buildings. A two-story loggia at the Villa Giustinian

19a Villa Cornaro

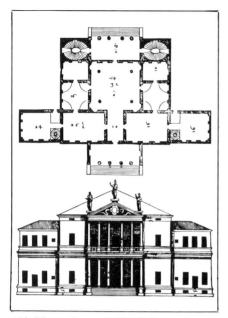

19b Plan, elevation (Book II, 1570)

19c Atrium (Book II, 1570)

in Roncade (c. 1511–1513, by Tullio Lombardo) was an immediate precedent. Palladio would have known the Villa Giustinian, as it was near the Barco of Caterina Cornaro, former Queen of Cyprus, whose brother's descendants were Palladio's patrons at Piombino Dese.[1]

Palladio was careful to coordinate pragmatic concerns with his spatial ideas for the Villa Cornaro. He planned no *barchesse* for the site but designed the beautiful seven-arched bridge leading to the garden gate. The inset loggia and oval stairs on the garden facade afford protection

19d View from garden

19e Sala

from southern exposure. On the interior the four-columned atrium provides structural support for the *sala* above. The beams spanning the columns give direction to the cubic space, reinforcing the axial connection to the garden.

This was the first villa in which Palladio integrated the service wings (executed after his death) within the building mass. Their junction remains awkward three-dimensionally, although they impart a clear hierarchy to the major facades. That facing the street has the quality of an extended wall with a projecting open porch, while that to the garden gives the impression of a smaller pavilion framed by recessed service wings. The Villa Cor-naro engages the context of the town with tremendous power, and simultaneously gathers the garden and park beyond into its domain.

[1] A statue of Queen Caterina is included among those of distinguished family members in the Villa Cornaro atrium, and her country retreat near Altivole, with its vast ornamental *barchesse*, undoubtedly influenced Palladio's nonutilitarian use of the same motif in several of his rural villas.

20a Villa Pisani

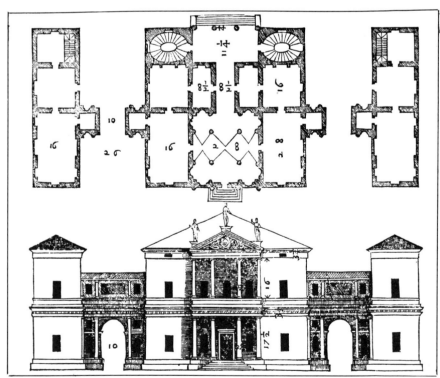

20b Plan, elevation (Book II, 1570)

20. VILLA PISANI - PLACCO
Porta Padova, Montagnana (Padova)
Book II, plate 35   1552/3–55

Private. Visits can be arranged through the owner, Signora Francesca Placco. Tel. 0429/81368.

The Villa Pisani, designed for the Venetian nobleman Francesco Pisani, marks the beginning of Palladio's work for an expanded circle of patrons in the 1550s. It was built just outside the medieval walls of Montagnana, straddling the town moat. Construction progressed rapidly and was complete by 1555. Vittoria was responsible for the tympanum stucco decorations and the four seasons in the atrium.

This was Palladio's second villa to be constructed with two major living floors. It is included with his villas in the *Quattro Libri*, although the formal resemblance to the Palazzo Antonini in plan and elevation

20c View from garden

transcends this typological distinction. Indeed its location just outside the town's fortified walls accounts for the villa's urban character. The lateral wings in the *Quattro Libri* plate are elaborations of the original project, as they could not be accommodated on the site. The existing appendages are unrelated to his design.

Many themes explored at the Villa Pisani are related directly to those of the contemporary Villa Cornaro and Palazzo Antonini. The motif of a two-story entry loggia with crowning pediment is applied to the surface of the entry facade, expressing the interior spatial organization. The four-columned atrium is articulated with intersecting barrel vaults — a new plastic interpretation of the Vitruvian theme. An important cross-axis is introduced in the atrium by the position of the major vault, at right angles to the entry. Because there are two living floors, the stairs have greater prominence; for the sake of symmetry they are paired to either side of the inset garden loggia, as at Piombino Dese.

20d Moat

20e Sala

21. PALAZZO ANTONINI (BANCA D'ITALIA)
Via Palladio, Udine
Book II, plate 1   c. 1552?–56

It is not certain when Floriano Antonini engaged Palladio to design his palace in Udine; based on stylistic evidence, it was probably not before 1552. Palladio visited Udine in 1556 while construction was under way. Work stopped after completion of the basic fabric, including definition of the major facades. The palace was finished in the 1590s or later, with substantive deviations from Palladio's original design. The service wing indicated in the *Quattro Libri* plate was never realized. Martino Fischer executed the interior decorations in the seventeenth century.

Although the character of the original context is uncertain, the site conditions of the Palazzo Antonini — fronting a major street with a large suburban garden to the rear — predicate its formal relationship to Palladio's contemporaneous palace-villas, the Villa Cornaro and Villa Pisani. The entry facade is based on themes established at the Villa Pisani, although here the entry motif is articulated with engaged columns and heavy rustication.

21a Palazzo Antonini

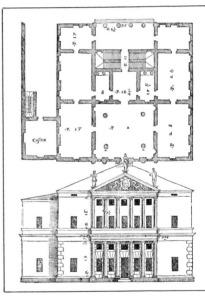

21b Plan, elevation (Book II, 1570)

The four-columned atrium is again the pivotal room of the plan, and its importance is announced on the urban facade by the expression of the upper windows, a motif repeated in the major *sala* above. An inset double loggia facing the garden marks the elaborate entry from the park. A symmetrical range of stairs has been added between the garden loggia and atrium, significantly modifying Palladio's spatial intentions.

21d View from garden

21c Sala

22. VILLA SEREGO - INNOCENTI
Santa Sophia di Pedemonte (Verona)
Book II, plate 49

1552/3?–69

Private. Ask custodian for permission to visit exterior.

The Villa Serego is Palladio's only surviving villa organized around a courtyard with no dominant central pavilion.[1] The date of the project is uncertain, although it was not begun before 1552, when the patron, Marc'Antonio Serego, inherited the property. His ancestors acquired the villa in 1313, at which time it consisted of a palace with dovecotes, courts, annexes, a chapel, vineyards, and illustrious gardens dating from Roman times. A series of improvements during the intervening period left the configuration in an irresolute state, and Marc'Antonio may have called on Palladio to coordinate the various elements within an overall design as early as 1552. Construction was under way between 1565 and 1569, when the powerful two-story loggia of heavily rusticated columns was built to organize the preexisting structures into a coherent whole.

Only a portion of Palladio's ambitious project was realized. The U-shaped loggia corresponds to half the rectangular courtyard of the published plan. Although the cornice that completes its open end seems to preclude extension, column bases in the other half of the courtyard were described by Muttoni (1740) and remained in place until the nineteenth century. Palladio may have been responsible only for the loggia, since the column spacing does not correspond to the fenestration of the adjoining walls. Recent tests indicate that portions of the outer wall were constructed in the 1380s, and the courtyard walls date from the 1530s — well before Palladio's intervention.

22a Villa Serego

22b Villa della Torre, Fumane

22c View from proposed exedra

The published version of the Villa Serego is unresolved volumetrically, notably in the exedra. While discrepancies often exist between Palladio's buildings and his idealized illustrations, the lack of three-dimensional resolution in this design has led scholars to speculate that the drawings were made in haste to include the project in his 1570 publication; however, the same lack of resolve exists in the built fragment.

The spatial organization and surface articulation of the Villa Serego are unusual for a Palladian villa, although examples of both exist in his work. The plan

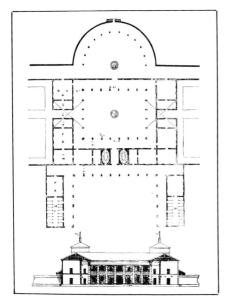

22d Plan, section (Book II, 1570)

is related thematically to the open-court plan of the contemporary Villa Mocenigo at Dolo, built between 1554 and 1563; these two projects probably inspired Palladio's subsequent redefinition of the Villa Thiene for publication in the *Quattro Libri*. Palladio's reconstruction of the House of the Ancients is a formal source of inspiration for these villas, and, significantly, in the *Quattro Libri* Palladio refers to the ancient origins of the Santa Sophia site as if to justify his use of that spatial idea.

The Villa Serego is often described as an anomaly in Palladio's work. While its formal organization initiated what was to become a recurring theme, its surface articulation is indeed unusual in Palladio's villa vocabulary. A similar rusticated pier forms the back gate of the Villa Pisani at Bagnolo, which was built during the second phase of Palladio's involvement there in the 1560s. However, at Santa Sophia he was probably inspired by a local precedent, the Villa della Torre in Fumane, built for Giulio della Torre in the 1550s by an unknown architect.[2]

The Villa della Torre is organized around an open courtyard, articulated with heavily rusticated piers. Furthermore, both villas use the same local yellow stone from a quarry owned by the Serego family. Palladio often adopted local architectural idioms in his projects, and so it is not surprising that he would

71

22e Column detail

22f Villa Pisani gate

have been influenced by the Villa della Torre. Its similarity to his reconstruction of the House of the Ancients must have intrigued Palladio and possibly prompted his entire series of courtyard villas.

Unlike the courtyard of the Villa della Torre, that of the Villa Serego is typologically derived from the urban palace, suitably transformed for the Veronese countryside. It is similar to the Villa Mocenigo of the same period, although Palladio's innovative solution for the Palazzo della Torre in Verona should also be borne in mind.[3] His overriding concern for the inherent meanings in architectural form allowed Palladio to set aside preconceptions about building types and to invent new types appropriate to the problem at hand. These were adapted to the symbolic aspirations of his patrons as well as to the particular circumstances of program and site.

[1] A second courtyard villa for the Mocenigo family at Dolo, built between 1554 and 1563, was demolished in 1835. A third, the Villa Repeta at Campiglia, was destroyed by fire in 1672, and may not have corresponded to the plan illustrated in the *Quattro Libri*.
[2] Bartolomeo Ridolfi was responsible for the fireplaces and stucco decorations of the Villa della Torre. The chapel is by Sanmicheli; inscribed on its bell is the date 1558, the year in which the patron died. Marc'Antonio Serego married into the della Torre family; his brother-in-law, Giovanni Battista della Torre, was Palladio's patron in Verona.
[3] The relationship to Sansovino's Villa Garzoni at Pontecasale is probably incidental.

22g Aerial view

23. PALAZZO VALMARANA - BRAGA
Corso Fogazzaro, 16, Vicenza
Book II, plates 11, 12   1554-58, 1565/6-71

In 1554 Giovanni Alvise Valmarana commissioned Palladio to make improvements to a large house that had been in his family since 1487. The property included a courtyard and garden, extending to stables near the Church of Ss. Filippo e Giacomo, and an adjacent house, portions of which are visible in the courtyard of the seventeenth-century Palazzo Valmarana-Rossi. The patron died in 1558 and Palladio revised the project for Valmarana's widow, Isabella Nogarola.

Construction was undertaken between 1565 and 1571 by Pietro da Nanto, although no effort was made to build the apartments overlooking the garden or the stables. Rather than complete Palladio's ambitious design, in 1593 the patron's son, Leonardo Valmarana, purchased an adjoining house facing the Corso (Palazzo Braschi-Brunelli) and connected it to the courtyard of his incomplete palace.

23a Palazzo Valmarana

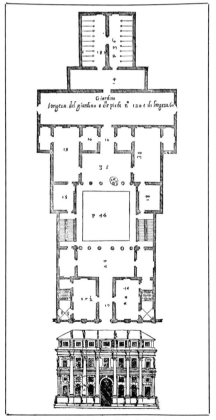

23b Plan, elevation (Book II, 1570)

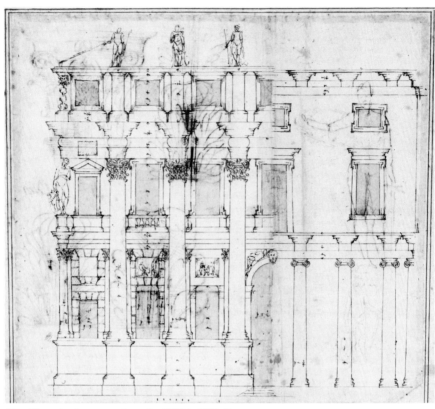

23c Elevation/courtyard study (RIBA XVI,4)

Due to extensive modifications to the building fabric and reconstruction of the interior after bomb damage in 1945, it is now impossible to determine the extent of Palladio's original intervention. He was responsible for regularizing the plan and constructing a new facade and a portion of the courtyard. The sculptural decorations included in Palladio's facade drawing (RIBA XVI,4) were executed in the 1580s by Domenico Fontana.

In the *Quattro Libri* illustration Palladio idealized the actual solution, rationalizing the earlier structures within a coherent composition. The formal layering of spaces in plan is reminiscent of his reconstruction of the House of the Ancients. Certain aspects of the plan are unusual for Palladio, including the nar-row entry passage leading to the courtyard and the *sala* over the rear loggia facing the garden (unexecuted). The entry no doubt reflects the preexisting construction.

The street facade, completed essentially as designed, is the most impressive aspect of the Palazzo Valmarana. The giant order of pilasters in the central bays produces a monumentality that is striking in this street of Renaissance facades. This order is interwoven with a smaller order that extends the entire width of the facade, in deference to the scale of the adjoining buildings. Palladio varied his system of openings in the end bays in a manner similar to the Palazzo Thiene courtyard. The sculptural figures, which cap the end pilasters, extend to the height of the giant order, emphasizing the dis-

23d Courtyard

tinction between the two systems. The articulation of the orders creates a sense of compression toward the center of the facade, reinforcing the entry and contributing to the scenographic effect.

Although he may have been aware of Michelangelo's use of a giant order at St. Peter's or his design for the Campidoglio, Palladio probably arrived at his solution independent of Michelangelo's influence. The combination of orders of different scales is suggested in several of Palladio's drawings of antiquities, such as his hypothetical reconstruction of the Temple of Assisi (RIBA XVI,9v). Indeed, the use of orders on the Palazzo Valmarana facade was anticipated in Palladio's brilliant series of Venetian church facades from the late 1550s.

23e Facade detail

24. VILLA THIENE (barchessa)
Cicogna di Villafranca Padovana (Padova)
Book II, plate 45   1554?–56

Private. Ask permission to visit.

In 1539 the Thiene family acquired property in Cicogna and made improvements to it, so that by 1546 the villa included a stately home with barn, dovecote, orchard, threshing floor, and gardens. It was probably in the mid-1550s that Francesco Thiene asked Palladio to design an elaborate new villa complex, of which the courtyard was marked out and a single *barchessa* erected before construction was interrupted by the patron's premature death in 1556.

The *barchessa* has five bays, one more than the published plan indicates. A

design drawing (RIBA XVII,20) showing a pediment (unexecuted) over the central bay may be the work of Palladio's nephew, Marc'Antonio. Palladio's illustration in the *Quattro Libri* is indebted to the Villa Badoer, which suggests that he may have modified his original design for publication. The combination of a large palace-villa with extensive service wings is not found in any executed work.

Despite the incomplete construction, new roads were built at Cicogna, laid out by Palladio in accordance with his architectural intentions.

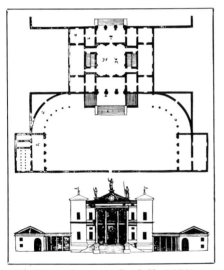

24b Plan, elevation (Book II, 1570)

24a Villa Thiene, barchessa

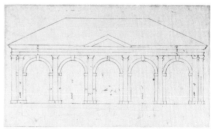

24c Barchessa *study (RIBA XVII,20b)*

25. PALAZZO POIANA*
Contra S. Tomaso, 30, Vicenza   1555?

The Palazzo Poiana is a fragment of an ambitious scheme whose total form can only be imagined. It is tentatively attributed to Palladio on stylistic grounds and on the basis of his established professional connections with the patron, Bonifacio Poiana, who engaged Palladio to design his villa at Poiana in the mid-1540s. The villa was Poiana's major residence until he returned to Vicenza in 1555, when Palladio's project for the palace may have been initiated. We know nothing of the circumstances of the commission or the reason for halting construction, although Poiana was living in the palace when he wrote his will in 1576.

The executed facade segment is composed forcefully and related to an earlier study for the Palazzo da Porto (RIBA XVII,9r); a dominant order of Corinthian pilasters unites the *piano nobile* and attic stories above a rusticated base — as in the da Porta study. At the Palazzo Poiana, the sharp line separating these zones and the lack of integration between them are not characteristic of Palladio's mature work. The narrow band of rustication separating the entry portico from the elongated window above seems inadequate. Similar articulation at the Palazzo Poiana sul Corso, also attributed to Palladio, is more likely the work of Domenico Groppino.

The window interrupting the cornice may have resulted from modifications in the seventeenth century, when the adjoining palace was built by another Bonifacio Poiana; this window aligns with those in the attic of the newer building. However, at the Palazzo Schio, where Palladio developed variations on several themes established in the Palazzo Poiana, he also inserted windows in the cornice.

It is likely that Palladio was the author of the Palazzo Poiana, which may have been built without much direct supervision during his prolonged periods of absence from Vicenza in the 1550s.

25a Palazzo Poiana

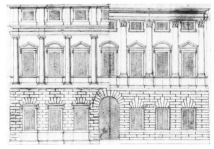

25b Palazzo da Porto, study (RIBA XVII,9r)

26. ARCO BOLLANI
Piazza della Libertà, Udine   1556, 1563

The Arco Bollani was erected to celebrate
the end of the plague in 1556 and to honor
the efforts of the Venetian Lieutenant
Domenico Bollani to aid the city of
Udine.[1] Palladio's role in its design is
undocumented; the attribution is based on
his later involvement in the reorganization
of the surrounding area and on stylistic
evidence.

The surface treatment of the Arco
Bollani is related to the Palazzo Antonini
entry motif and the ground-floor loggia of
the Palazzo Municipale in Feltre of 1557;
it is also similar to Palladio's gate in San
Daniele del Friuli.

The arch was originally isolated from
the public piazza it now faces. In 1563 the
Udine City Council asked Palladio to
strengthen the visual relationship between the Piazza della Libertà, the Arco

26a Arco Bollani

Bollani, and the castle on the hill above.
It is assumed that Palladio was called to
Udine for this small commission because
of his involvement with the original construction of the arch.

Several public buildings in the corner
of the piazza were demolished and replaced by a short road. By this intervention Palladio made the arch an urban fea-
ture of the public square; at the same time
he clarified its visual and symbolic connection to the castle above, as the arch
signifies access to the medieval fortifica-
tion.

[1] In 1567 Bollani, as Bishop of Brescia, sought Palladio's advice about rebuilding the Cathedral of
Brescia, although nothing came of that ambitious
venture.

27. VILLA BADOER
Fratta Polesine (Rovigo)
Book II, plate 31   1556/7–63

Visit: March through September: Tuesday through Saturday 9–12 and 3–7. (October through February: 10–12 and 2–5). Tel. 0425/68122.

Between 1545 and 1548 the Venetian nobleman Francesco Badoer acquired property near Fratta Polesine through the death of his brother-in-law, Giorgio Loredan. By 1556 Badoer purchased the site of an older castle to build his residence close to the village, and in the following year Palladio's project was under construction. Set in the flat landscape of Rovigo, the Villa Badoer faces the village of Fratta across the River Scortico, which was the water route from Venice. The direct relationship to the river has been modified by the banks elevated to control flooding in this low-lying region.

In many ways the Villa Badoer represents the quintessential Palladian villa: its plan is related to that at Poiana, with an elongated central *sala* similar to the *portego* of the Venetian palace; the entry porch is recessed as at the Villa Emo; and the curving *barchesse* define the entry court and frame the elevated central pavilion scenographically.

These are the only curved loggias in Palladio's executed work, although he proposed similar elements for the Villa Thiene at Cicogna, the Villa Trissino at Meledo, and the Villa Mocenigo sul Brenta. The *barchesse* at Fratta are symbolic rather than pragmatic, initiating the spatial sequence that leads from the entry court, through the central residential pavilion, to the walled garden court

27a Villa Badoer

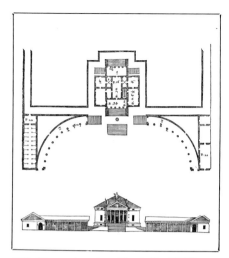

27d Side facade

27b Plan, elevation (Book II, 1570)

beyond. This triadic composition characteristic of Palladian villas is similar to the spatial organization of his palaces and churches.

At the Villa Badoer Palladio refined the primary architectural means, abstracting the essence of the forms, so that the meaning of the whole is enhanced by the independent treatment of the parts. The Tuscan order of the curving loggias contrasts with the Ionic order of the entry portico. The junction between the elements is abrupt; a high podium, interrupting the *barchesse* and extending around to the garden, elevates the central block in a manner that transcends the practical requirements of a service basement, as if to accentuate the owner's status. This theme is interpreted metaphorically in the fresco decorations by Giallo Fiorentino. The entry portico originally included the coat of arms of the Badoer and Loredan families in its tympanum. The rear facade is incomplete, and the side facades lack compositional unity, reinforcing the primacy of the public, frontal view.

27c Entry view

28. PALAZZO MUNICIPALE*
Piazza Maggiore, Feltre (Belluno) 1557–58

Palladio may have been responsible for the ground-floor loggia of the municipal headquarters in Feltre. Local tradition links him to the project, although his involvement is undocumented. Efforts to rebuild the headquarters of the Feltre City Council in 1518, 1543, and again in 1548 were besieged by economic difficulties. Finally, between 1557 and 1558, the ground floor of the present loggia was built. Palladio may have been called in by the Venetian administrator Francesco Cividale, a Vicentine active in the public life of his native city, who was responsible for this project in Feltre.

The upper floors of the building were completed between 1559 and 1562 in a manner different from the loggia, possibly to the design of Giambattista Tagliapietra. It is unclear why Palladio's activity on the building would have been terminated and another architect called in, particularly because construction appears to have proceeded without interruption.

The surface treatment and materials of the loggia are related to the Palazzo Antonini and Arco Bollani in Udine; all three were under construction at the same time.

29. S. MARIA MAGGIORE (entablature, drum, cupola)
Piazza del Duomo, Vicenza 1557–59, 1564–74

The main chapel of the Cathedral of Vicenza was reconstructed, beginning in 1482, to the design of Lorenzo da Bologna. The work was repeatedly interrupted by financial and political problems and was still incomplete in the mid-sixteenth century. Palladio was responsible for the entablature and drum of the apse, erected in 1557. Construction of the cupola was not begun until 1564, by which time Palladio may have revised an earlier design, following his experiences at S. Giorgio Maggiore and Brescia Cathedral.

29a Cathedral of S. Maria Maggiore

30. VILLA FOSCARI ("La Malcontenta")

Gambarare di Mira (Venice)

Book II, plate 33   c. 1558–60

Visit: May through October: Tuesday and Saturday 9–12. For group visits on other days, telephone in advance. Tel. 041/5470012.

The Villa Foscari was conceived as a suburban retreat on the Brenta Canal, not far from Venice, for the brothers Nicolo and Alvise Foscari. Although it is uncertain when Palladio began the project, we know that construction was nearly complete at the time of Nicolo's death in 1560. The building corresponds to Palladio's illustration in the *Quattro Libri*. There were originally no outbuildings; those built in the seventeenth century, including a small chapel, were later demolished.

The Villa Foscari extends the palace-villa theme found at Piombino Dese and Montagnana. It is raised on an exceptionally high base, since the low-lying site precluded sinking the service basement. The increased height of the mass and the uniform rustication of the exterior contribute to the villa's urban character. The direct juxtaposition of central *sala* and garden view is an innovation to the type. The thermal window on the central axis extends the room visually to the walled garden and the landscape beyond, although access to the garden is indirect, via the front porch.

The relationship to the landscape is enhanced in the decorative scheme that celebrates the glories of country living and the owners' status. Zelotti and India painted the interior frescoes around 1561,

30a Villa Foscari

the year Battista Franco died while executing the "Fall of the Giants" in a side room. The villa was restored in the twentieth century and currently is owned by architects descended from the original patrons.

Several aspects of the Villa Foscari are taken directly from other Palladian villas: the plan repeats that intended for the Villa Chiericati at Vancimuglio, and the pattern of openings in the garden facade is similar to the entry facade of the Villa Zen. These are assimilated with other familiar Palladian themes and brought to an exceptional level of refinement.

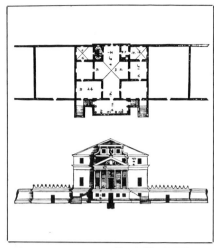

30b Plan, elevation (Book II, 1570)

30c View from garden

31. VILLA ZEN
Donegal di Cessalto (Treviso)
Book II, plate 32   c.1558-66?

Private and uninhabited. Ask farm administrator for permission to visit.

This remote villa was built for Marco Zen, who was mayor of Vicenza between 1558 and 1559. Palladio's commission possibly dates from the same period. The villa existed by 1566, although it is difficult to date stylistically due to its deteriorated condition and modifications to the primary facade. It is uncertain whether the outbuildings and colonnades described in the *Quattro Libri* were realized in the sixteenth century; those noted by Muttoni (1740) have since been destroyed.

The villa faces the Piovan Canal, which served as the primary means of arrival. The facade toward the farm court is unresolved; it originally included a thermal window lighting the central *sala*.

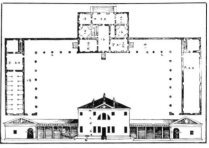

31b Plan, elevation (Book II, 1570)

A beautiful triple-arched loggia faces the garden. Despite the affinities of these elements with the Villa Pisani at Bagnolo and the Villa Saraceno respectively, the context in which they are used is quite different. Indeed, there is a curious inversion of these facades: the inset loggia, a

31a Villa Zen

theme that usually denotes entry, faces the garden, while the entry facade on the courtyard is articulated more subtly.The pattern of openings is similar to that facing the garden at the Villa Foscari, and seems to anticipate the Venetian facade of le Zitelle. This suggests that Palladio used the experiments in this remote villa as ground for further invention.

31c View from garden

32. VILLA TRISSINO - FACCHINI
Meledo di Sarego (Vicenza)
Book II, plate 43   1558?-62?

Private. Ask permission to visit.

Little is known of the circumstances surrounding Palladio's commission to design a villa for the brothers Francesco and Lodovico Trissino in Meledo. Palladio may have begun work on a new residential complex for their country estate in 1558, while he was preparing plans to rebuild the family's palace in Vicenza (unexecuted). This date conforms to the stylistic evidence.

An earlier dovecote and wall were built on the property between 1553 and 1554, and, according to an inscription, the frescoes in the base of the tower were undertaken from 1575 to 1576. The work in progress cited in Palladio's *Quattro Libri* description probably included a loggia with Tuscan columns attached to the

earlier dovecote and the segment of a second loggia across the court. These and a rusticated entry gate are all that were executed of this elaborate project, on which construction was probably halted before the death of Lodovico Trissino in 1563.

The existing fragments do not correspond precisely to the *Quattro Libri* illustration, although an adequate site survey has never been made. The published design is an elaboration of the original project; it conforms generally to the circumstances of the site. (The unbuilt portions would extend to just below the church that now adjoins the property.) The plan was inspired by Palladio's fanciful reconstruction of the Forum and Sanctuary of Fortu-

32a Villa Trissino, entry gate and loggia

32b Preexisting tower and wall

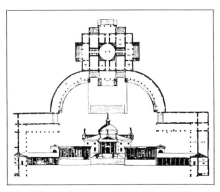

32c Plan, elevation (Book II, 1570)

na Primigenia at Palestrina — also interpreted as the Temple of Hercules Victor at Tivoli (RIBA VIII,11r and IX,7 and 8). Palladio adapted the spatial idea from the steep site of the original to the gentle terrain of Meledo by abstracting from his plan drawing.

The Villa Trissino is an elaboration of the centralized villa type realized only in the Villa Rotonda. The hierarchical distinction between front and sides (noted primarily in the Rotonda interior) is externalized in Palladio's woodcut of the Villa Trissino through projecting porches on the primary axis and recessed loggias to the sides. The primacy of the entry axis is reinforced by the alternating rectilinear and curving *barchesse* that step up the site and scenographically frame the house itself — an elaboration of ideas initiated at the Villa Badoer.

33. CASA COGOLLO (facade)
Corso Andrea Palladio, 163, Vicenza   1559–62

In 1559 the lawyer Pietro Cogollo's application for citizenship in Vicenza was approved on condition that he improve the facade of his house. Muttoni (1740) first attributed the design to Palladio, although Scamozzi (1776–83) questioned the attribution; it is now generally accepted on the basis of Palladio's established connections with the patron as well as on stylistic grounds.[1] Palladio's involvement was confined to expanding the building toward the street; he was responsible for the loggia as well as the facade.

To rationalize the existing structure with its context, Palladio divided the facade into three horizontal and vertical zones. The ground-floor loggia is derived from a triumphal arch. At the *piano nobile* a large blank panel, which originally contained a fresco by Fasolo, reinforces the central emphasis of the triumphal arch

motif. By combining themes of centrality (triumphal arch, frescoed panel) with elements of linear continuity (loggia, cornice), Palladio asserted the individuality of the house while respecting the continuity of the street. In contrast to the repetitive rhythms of the adjacent facades, the cross-axis established by these centralizing motifs produces a monumental effect, imparting dignity to the otherwise modest palace.

Palladio compensated for the oblique view by the implied frontality of his facade. Its perceptual qualities are reinforced by the details; crisp molding profiles contrast with the simplicity of the wall surface, accentuated by the absence of window frames. In overall conception, and detail, the Casa Cogollo reveals Palladio's hand.

[1] Palladio frequently witnessed Cogollo's legal documents.

33a Casa Cogollo

33b Elevation (Scamozzi, 1761)

34a Villa Emo

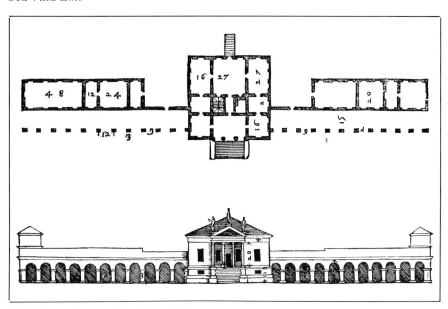

34b Plan, elevation (Book II, 1570)

90

34. VILLA EMO - CAPODILISTA

Fanzolo di Vedelago (Treviso)

Book II, plate 38   c. 1559–65

Visit: April through September: Tuesday and Saturday 3–7; October through March: Saturday and Sunday 2–6; groups of 15 or more by appointment. Tel. 0423/476334.

In 1539 Leonardo Emo di Alvise inherited a portion of the family property in Fanzolo from his uncle, a Venetian patrician. The land was acquired as part of an extensive effort by the Venetian nobility to develop the *terra firma* for agricultural use. Leonardo was seven years old at the time, and so it was not until around 1559 that he engaged Palladio to design a new residential complex for the estate. A description of the villa is included in a fragment of the *Quattro Libri* text drafted in 1561, indicating that the project was then under way.

The interior frescoes by Zelotti were executed between 1560 and 1565, so that the entire project was completed before the patron's marriage to Cornelia Grimani in 1565.

The villa corresponds to Palladio's illustrations in the *Quattro Libri*, although the dovecotes are indicated in elevation and not in plan. There are also discrepancies concerning the connection of the service wings to the central block in plan and elevation, and the built version does not correspond to either.

Palladio's design for the Villa Emo assembles formal themes from earlier villas in a new and compelling way. The central residential block is related to the Villa Badoer, and similar elongated *barchesse* were used at Maser. The ensemble is characterized by the autonomy of its parts: the central block, lateral wings, and dovecotes are articulated independently in plan and surface. The form of the *barchesse* may reflect a local vernacular type, exemplified in the pre-

34c Aerial view

Palladian villa at Cusignana di Arcade. Sanmicheli also built lateral *barchesse* at the Villa "La Soranza" in Treville di Castelfranco, completed by 1551 (of which only one outbuilding remains).

At Fanzolo the parallels between architecture and landscape are more pronounced than in Palladio's earlier villas. A long avenue of poplars along the central axis defines the approach; it is reiterated in the agricultural fields beyond the garden, where it extends as far as one can see. The landscaped entry axis is countered by the elongated service wings that spread perpendicularly. From the approach the poplars frame the lateral wings, which extend beyond one's field of vision. This endless quality is reinforced by the position of the dovecotes, pulled to the rear of the *barchesse* to terminate the garden facade. In contrast to the entry facade, that facing the garden can be viewed in its entirety and is treated as a series of interrupted volumes. These calculated visual effects are reinforced by the ramped entry stair, which elevates the ground plane to the main living floor. The

34d View toward entry

34e View from garden

raised central *sala* stands at the intersection of architecture and nature, a theme reinforced by the Zelotti frescoes that illustrate the glories of villa life.

While they function visually and symbolically, these elements serve pragmatic needs. The ramped entry stair was a surface for threshing grain, and the *barchesse* were intended as farm buildings; thus their functions are asymmetrically disposed in plan. Like those at the unfinished Villa Angarano, the *barchesse* are prominent. Their scenographic treatment contrasts with the utilitarian farm buildings across the modern road, added to serve the villa's expanding agricultural needs. Palladio exploited the power of his service wings to enhance his architectural intentions, and they were appropriately modified for residential use in the eighteenth century.

The calculated visual effects of the Villa Emo celebrate its importance as an agricultural center as well as the patron's aspirations. In the strength of its overall idea and its specific execution, the Villa Emo represents a new degree of integration at all scales of architectural concern.

34f Sala

35. REFECTORY OF SAN GIORGIO MAGGIORE (CINI FOUNDATION)

Isola di San Giorgio, Venice 1560–63

Visit: The Cini Foundation is private, but tours are organized occasionally. Check with the custodian.

As part of an extended program initiated in the 1520s to improve the Benedictine church and monastery of San Giorgio Maggiore, the abbot Girolamo Scrocchetto asked Palladio in 1560 to complete the refectory. Work on Palladio's project, including the wine store and kitchen, was completed in 1563.

An earlier proposal for the refectory had been partially constructed by the masons Battista and Simone in 1540. Their work was removed to give Palladio greater latitude in spatial definition. He derived the ceiling vaults and thermal windows, which originally marked the

cross-axis, from his studies of Roman baths.

Canera and Veronese produced the paintings that were originally in the refectory. Palladio may have collaborated with Veronese on the refectory seats. The painter's *Marriage at Cana* (now in the Louvre) visually extended the confined architectural space, suggesting that they discussed the relationship between the architecture and the painting.

The success of this modest project led to Palladio's commission to rebuild the church in 1564.

35a S. Giorgio Maggiore, refectory

36a S. Maria della Carita, cloister

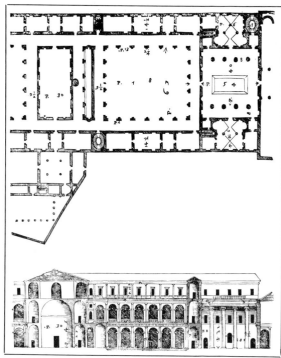

36b Plan, section (Book II, 1570)

36. MONASTERY OF S. MARIA DELLA CARITA (ACCADEMIA DI BELLE ARTI)

Venice

Book II, plates 20, 21, 22   1560–70

Visit: Ask permission of the custodian to visit the courtyard. The sacristy and oval staircase are closed to visitors.

In 1560 Palladio was asked to provide a master plan for the monastery of S. Maria della Carita, which consisted of a church and four courtyards formed by service buildings (within a walled cemetery). This was Palladio's first project in Venice to be realized, even in part, and it represents a significant event in the architectural life of the city. The compatibility of Palladio's historical interests with the Roman origins of the order may have prompted his appointment for this important commission.

Only a portion of Palladio's ambitious scheme was built, and a fire damaged part of the work in 1630. The surviving elements of his design include a segment of the cloister, the sacristy, and an adjoining oval staircase. In 1807 the building was modified to its present state to accommodate an art gallery.

Palladio's intentions for the project are known only through his illustration in the *Quattro Libri*, where he idealized the irregular site. The inspiration for the plan was his reconstruction of the House of the Ancients, which served as a model for the internal reorganization of the monastery. Palladio adapted his interpretation of the atrium, tablinum, and peristyle of the ancient house to a larger program, bringing added meaning to the complex. The plan displays a marked indifference to the existing street pattern by imposing an order that is directed inward, in keeping with the monastic community it was intended to serve.

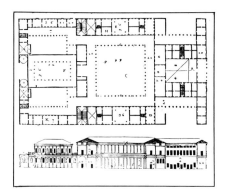

36c House

36d Cloister detail (Book II, 1570)

95

37. PALAZZO POIANA SUL CORSO (facade)*
Corso Andrea Palladio, Vicenza   1560?-61

In 1561 the City Council granted Vincenzo Poiana permission to renew the facade of his urban palace and join it to an adjacent building on the Corso; by 1566, when he wrote his will, the work was complete. Modern historians have suggested that Palladio was responsible for the renovation, although no documentation supports the attribution.

The facade resembles the earlier palace for Bonifazio Poiana (a cousin of the owner), attributed to Palladio on stylistic grounds; the visual evidence for the Palazzo Poiana sul Corso is less convincing. Each facade includes a heavily rusticated base with a smooth upper zone, articulated by giant Corinthian pilasters. The raised arches of the central doorways are also similar, although the treatment is less resolved in this later project. The protruding balconies, common to sixteenth-century Vicentine palace courtyards, are without precedent in Palladio's palace facades.

Despite its awkward qualities, the facade of the Palazzo Poiana sul Corso shows strong design intentions; it is most likely the work of a master mason such as Domenico Groppino, who frequently imitated Palladio's work.

37a Palazzo Poiana sul Corso

38. SAN FRANCESCO DELLA VIGNA (facade)
Campo di San Francesco della Vigna, Venice   1562–70?

In 1562 the Patriarch of Aquileia, Giovanni Grimani, asked Palladio to design a facade for the Church of San Francesco della Vigna. Daniele Barbaro probably influenced the selection of his protégé for this important commission.[1] It was Palladio's first executed church facade in Venice, with construction well advanced by 1566. The fundamental logic of his solution was to influence the design of ecclesiastical facades for centuries.

The church was built to the design of Sansovino, who in 1534 had been asked by Doge Andrea Gritti and a group of prominent noblemen to translate harmonic proportions into architectural form. The proportional relationships were diluted in the executed building, and work was halted before construction of Sansovino's facade began.

As in the Basilica, Palladio shifted his interest from the relationship between the architectural object and its context to the rational organization of the facade. He disregarded the irregular conditions of the site (now altered) and the corresponding proportions of the interior to concentrate on the problem of the church facade in the abstract. The solution shows Palladio's concern with demythologizing architectural form to enable its reinterpretation in a new context.

On the facade Palladio used orders of different scales to bring about compositional unity, a device he used at the Palazzo Valmarana, under construction between 1565 and 1571. At San Francesco della Vigna, by incorporating corre-

38a San Francesco della Vigna

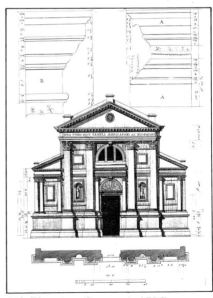

38b Elevation (Scamozzi, 1796)

97

sponding pediments, he resolved the divergent scales of nave and side aisles with a single architectural motif.[2] This solution was inspired by Palladio's drawings of antiquity, where he combined section and elevation with orders of different magnitudes on one sheet. He was to explore variations on this strategy in his important facades for San Giorgio Maggiore and the Redentore.

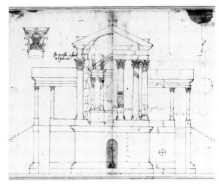

38c Temple of Clitumnus (RIBA XI,15r)

[1]In 1550 Grimani appointed Daniele Barbaro his successor as patriarch of Aquileia; Barbaro died before Grimani and never assumed the post.

[2]It is likely that Palladio first proposed combining pediments and orders of different scales in his facade for San Pietro di Castello, designed between 1557 and 1559, which was never executed and remains unknown. The facade of San Pietro di Castello was designed by Francesco Smeraldi and built between 1594 and 1596. Smeraldi may have been influenced by Palladio's design as well as by his executed facades for San Francesco della Vigna and the Redentore.

39. VILLA VALMARANA - SCAGNAROLI

Lisiera (Vicenza)

Book II, plate 42   c.1563–66, 1579–80

Visit: The villa is now a lamp store and can be visited during shop hours.

The Villa Valmarana was built for Gianfrancesco Valmarana, whose brother commissioned Palladio to design his palace in Vicenza. The patron was active in the public life of the city, and the family owned extensive property in Lisiera, where they controlled the watercourses. In about 1563 Gianfrancesco engaged Palladio to reconstruct the wooden bridge over the Tesina, and plans for refurbishing the villa may have begun at the same time.

Valmarana's death in 1566 interrupted construction, and the property was inherited by his nephew, Leonardo Valmarana, who made further improvements to the estate between 1579 and 1591. Because of the irresolute modifications to Palladio's design, it is uncertain when the

building was brought to its present form. The chapel was added in 1615; its attribution to Palladio (by Muttoni) is not accepted. The balusters in the attic windows are from the seventeenth century. The garden was redesigned in the early eighteenth century by Francesco Marina-

39b View toward entry

39a Villa Valmarana

li, who was responsible for the statues (1713–1715).

It is difficult to determine the site circumstances prior to Palladio's commission. In the *Quattro Libri* he describes two service courts, of which a medieval tower and attached *barchessa* remain; however, they are not integrated formally into the design. Palladio's residential block may include portions of earlier structures, although their extent is unknown since the villa sustained extensive damage during World War II and was almost completely rebuilt in 1969.

The executed building differs substantially from the version illustrated in the *Quattro Libri*, which is not a reliable indication of Palladio's intentions.

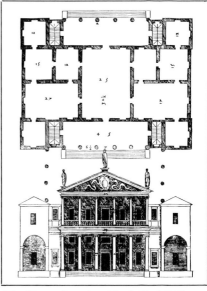

39c Plan, elevation (Book II, 1570)

40. PALAZZO PRETORIO

Piazza del Duomo, Cividale del Friuli (Udine)   1564–65

This civic palace in Cividale was built from Palladio's model between 1565 and 1586 without his direct supervision. Palladio, accompanied by the painter Federico Zuccari, traveled to Cividale for the inauguration of the work in 1565.

The ground-floor loggia of the Palazzo Pretorio marks Palladio's return to a theme initiated in the Palazzo Civena and developed in the Palazzo Chiericati and Basilica (see also the Palazzo Municipale in Feltre). The execution lacks the assured proportions and crisp detailing of his other projects because Palladio was not involved in its construction. The design reflects the scale and massing of the adjoining buildings, yet imparts dignity to the major civic space in a manner consistent with Palladio's spatial attitude.

40a Palazzo Pretorio

41a San Giorgio Maggiore

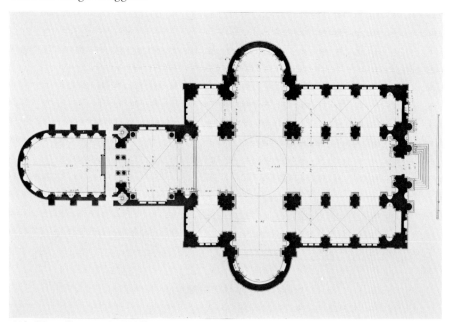

41b Plan (Scamozzi, 1783)

41. SAN GIORGIO MAGGIORE
Isola di San Giorgio, Venice   1564–80

In 1564 the recently installed abbot of San Giorgio Maggiore, Andrea Pampuro da Asolo, asked Palladio to replace the Benedictine church and renew the structure of the existing monastery. A building program initiated in the 1520s led to renewing the older parts of the church, on which work continued until 1550, and construction of Palladio's refectory between 1560 and 1563. The decision to alter the building program in progress probably resulted from liturgical modifications made by the Council of Trent in 1563, although the desire to convey a modern public image and to express the order's substantial wealth may also have been motives.

Construction of the new church began in 1566 and was incomplete at the time of Palladio's death in 1580. Those parts realized without his supervision include the choir (from 1583), high altar (1592), facade (1607–1611), and Cloister of the Cypresses (1579–1613).

The original church conformed to the contemporary Benedictine practice of a longitudinal nave with side aisles and chapels, terminated by a triple apse, with a transept surmounted by three cupolas. This was set behind a forecourt bounded by small, low buildings at the water's edge. The rest of the island was undeveloped at the time. Palladio retained the bell tower, which had been remodeled in the Renaissance, and it was rebuilt after collapsing in 1776.

The new church is oriented like its

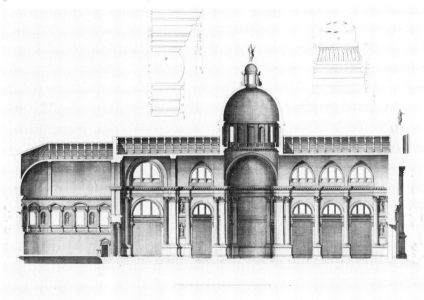

41c Section (Scamozzi, 1783)

41d View toward entry

41e Nave

predecessor, though set closer to the water, facing an open *campo*. Its innovative internal organization consists of three major elements: a longitudinal nave with domical crossing, a square presbytery containing the altar, and an apsidal choir. Each is articulated discretely and set at a different level. The choir is visually isolated by a columnar screen that separates the monks from the rest of the congregation. The nave, presbytery, and choir are united by their direct juxtaposition and axial alignment. Diffused light and subtle variations in color and detailing contribute to a visual continuity between the elements.

The organization of nave and presbytery around a domical crossing modifies the traditional basilican plan to a more centralized form, an ideal preferred by Renaissance theorists but realized infrequently due to liturgical considerations. Without the choir, the plan is a modified Latin cross. The symbolic program is complex. In the fusion of a temple form on the exterior with the basilican and

Latin cross organization of the interior, Palladio combined antique precedents with Renaissance formal ideals.

Palladio's facade, executed after his death, departs significantly from an early design drawing (RIBA XIV,12), which indicates a freestanding portico with columns extending to the ground. In contrast to the former church, which was introspective in character, the early proposal heightens the church's visibility from across the lagoon.[1] This approach, which afforded no opportunity to integrate the nave and side aisles, was ultimately abandoned.

In the executed facade Palladio used pedimented orders of two different scales to reflect the interior spatial hierarchy. He introduced the smaller order in the zone of the side aisles and carried it across

41f Aerial view

the central zone of the nave, where the giant order dominates. The two zones are discrete yet united by the a-b-a-b-a rhythm of the orders. This design is more subtle than that originally proposed, leading some scholars to speculate that it was modified, perhaps by Vincenzo Scamozzi, after Palladio's death. However, Palladio may have preferred the adopted design because it reflects the interior organization and articulation. It indicates his growing concern for continuity between the interior and exterior.

41g Cloister

[1]This aim was enhanced by the demolition of the adjoining houses in 1609 at the request of the Doge; their demise had been planned from 1521.

42. PALAZZO SCHIO - VACCARI (facade)
Contra S. Marco, 39, Vicenza   1565-66

Private. Ask permission to visit.

In 1565 Bernardo Schio asked Palladio to
design the facade of his house, which
Schio had built (or at least modified) to his
own design between 1561 and 1563. Despite the patron's death in 1566, the
facade was completed the following year.
In 1825 the inscription was added, and
the attic windows that originally interrupted the cornice were blocked in.

   The design imparts strength and dignity to a modest urban house. The primary reading of a two-story structure with
rusticated base and smooth *piano nobile*
soon gives over to a more complex under-
standing. The elongated *piano nobile* windows give a sense of compression to the
facade, an effect Palladio countered by
flattening the keystones over the ground-
floor windows and elongating those over
the arched basement windows. He reinforced the tension between the two major
zones by inserting the plinths of the *piano
nobile* columns, which are smooth, within
the rusticated zone of the base. The Palazzo Poiana may have been an early study of
similar themes.

42a Palazzo Schio

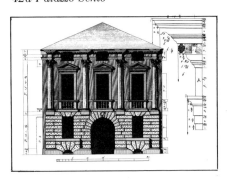

42b Elevation (Scamozzi, 1796)

43. VILLA ALMERICO - VALMARANA ("La Rotonda")
Vicenza

Book II, plate 13   c. 1565/6–69

Visit: Grounds, 15 March to 15 October, Tuesday through Thursday 10–12 and 3–6; other hours by appointment. Interiors can be visited on Wednesdays. Tel. 0444/321793.

The Villa Rotonda was conceived as a country residence for Paolo Almerico, a papal prelate. Upon returning to Vicenza in 1566 after many years in Rome, Almerico sold his palace with the intention of moving to his property just outside the city. Construction proceeded quickly, and by 1569 the building was inhabited. Palladio may have included this project with his urban palaces in the *Quattro Libri* because it was built just outside the city without the appendages of a working farm. With no need for storing grain, the attic originally provided "a place to walk round the hall"; however, it was subdivided in the eighteenth century.[1]

Construction was incomplete at the time of Palladio's death, and Scamozzi supervised the remaining work on the dome and exterior stairs. He was also responsible for the outbuilding, added in 1620 at a lower level. The statues at the entry stairs were completed by Lorenzo Rubini before 1570; the fireplaces are by Ridolfi (1577); the stuccoes in the cupola and ceilings of the main rooms are by Rubini, Ruggero Bascape, and Domenico Fontana (1581). Later additions to the decorative scheme include frescoes by Alessandro Maganza in the west and south rooms (1599–1600) and the lower frescoes in the central room and halls by Dorigny (1680–1687). The statues on the acroteria and garden fountain are by G. B. Albanese (1600), who later added the garden entrance from the Strada della

43a Villa Rotonda

Riviera (1629).

The site seems to have inspired Palladio's most unusual villa, for the Rotonda is his only freestanding centralized pavilion. Situated on top of a hill, it is framed on three sides by the cultivated fields of Monte Berico rising above at a distance. The original entry is still visible from the road below on the fourth side. Palladio

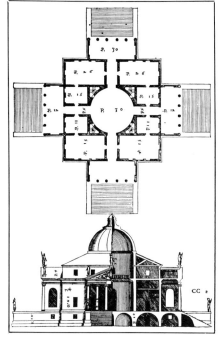

43b Plan, elevation (Book II, 1570)

describes the site as a "theater," and he justifies repeating the entry portico on all four faces to take advantage of the beautiful views. The Villa Rotonda *appears* to be conceived as an isolated object, independent of its site, due to its centralized form and the lack of connected outbuildings. However, from the original entry the planted fields of Monte Berico frame the building, linking it scenographically to the site as securely as the *barchesse* of other Palladian villas.

The exterior massing is reflected in the central *sala*, which is circular in plan and capped by a dome. It is Palladio's only major room that lacks both direct access to the secondary rooms and exterior exposure, save through the *oculus* of the dome. Palladio never again used this religious form in a secular context in his built work, though he included a circular *sala* in the plan of the Villa Trissino. At the Rotonda he used the dome not only in response to the unique qualities of the site, but also as a reference to the patron's position.

The dome is indebted to the Pantheon; its *oculus* was originally open, and a drain in the floor of the central *sala* led to a well in the basement. The dome illustrated in the *Quattro Libri* would have rendered explicit the building's religious connotations. The executed dome is more in keeping with Palladio's overall conception; its form and siting correspond to his reconstruction of the Roman theater at Verona (RIBA IX,10). The building itself is quite modest; its conception in relation to the site gives "La Rotonda" the grandeur that has made it seem the culmination of Palladio's villa architecture. It was to be his last executed villa.

[1]*Book II*, 41.

43c Sala

44. LOGGIA DEL CAPITANIATO
Piazza dei Signori, Vicenza   c. 1565/71–72

Palladio's Loggia del Capitaniato was constructed in 1572 as an appendage to the Palazzo del Capitaniato, built in 1404 in the present Contra del Monte as headquarters for the Venetian military. It replaced a single-story loggia that formed a side court of the palace, which, by 1571, had deteriorated and required rebuilding. An inscription under the side balcony affirms Palladio's authorship.

The Loggia del Capitaniato differs formally and programmatically from the original structure. It is a public building, monumental in scale, oriented toward the Piazza dei Signori. The loggia includes three open bays on the ground floor, from which public proclamations were read,

and a large hall above, accessible through the older palace. (The present stairs were added in the early nineteenth century.)

Muttoni (1740) and Scamozzi (1776) both state that construction was incomplete. They suggest that the original design consisted of seven bays extending to the Contra Cavour, and scholars have also argued convincingly that five bays were intended. However, the loggia as built is *formally* complete and does not imply lateral extension. The reason for their hypotheses may lie elsewhere.

In 1565 the City Council purchased all the houses and shops to the left of the original loggia to build a second loggia and council chamber to enhance the city's

44a Loggia del Capitaniato

44b Plan, elevation (Muttoni, 1760)

main piazza. Although nothing came of this ambitious venture, Palladio may have designed a loggia that remained unrealized for financial reasons. (If so, he did not include it in the *Quattro Libri*.) In 1571, when it became a matter of urgency to repair the loggia of the Palazzo del Capitaniato, Palladio could have adapted his earlier design to the adjoining site.

Modification of an earlier design would account for the loggia's rapid execution. While the city may have intended to extend the building once funds were available, Palladio designed a three-bay version that, with the palace, could stand alone. In 1928 expansion to five bays was actually approved, leading to the demolition of the adjoining houses. Except for the end facade added in the 1930s, construction was never resumed, leaving the present irresolute configuration of the urban piazza.

The thematic break between the facade toward the piazza and that facing the side street has been cited as evidence of a late change in design, particularly since the decorative treatment of the side facade commemorates the Venetian victory over the Turks at Lepanto in October 1571. The battle was at its height in April of that year when the plans for the loggia were completed and construction begun. Yet the formal integration of the two facades is evidence *against* a late design change. It is more reasonable to assume that the theme of a loggia on the piazza was combined with the more honorific theme of a triumphal arch on the side street to amplify the primary orientation of the Venetian official's residence. Though the major architectural themes and many details of the two facades differ considerably, unity is maintained by the density of decoration and transformation of architectural motifs from one facade to the other.

The controversies over the intended loggia length and its design chronology

44c View from piazza

44d Side elevation (Scamozzi, 1761)

have obscured the achievement of the architecture itself. This was Palladio's first construction to maintain the independence of front and side facades without sacrificing the integrity of the whole. Although the Loggia del Capitaniato is without precedent in Palladio's work, it is a powerful urban gesture, indicating the robust, inventive quality of his late work.

44e Facade detail

45. PONTE COPERTO
Via Angarano, Bassano del Grappa (Vicenza)
Book III, plate 6   1568/9–70

In 1567 the wooden bridge over the Brenta at Bassano was destroyed in a flood, and the following year the Venetian Senate approved funds for its reconstruction. The Bassano City Council asked Palladio to design the new bridge in the same form as its predecessor. He modified the proportions of the earlier structure to conform to Renaissance ideals. The original bridge had five supports, designed to withstand the pressure of high flood waters; Palladio reduced his supports to four. Construction was completed in 1570, and, despite repeated damage in the intervening centuries, the bridge has always been repaired to Palladio's design, with minor technical changes.

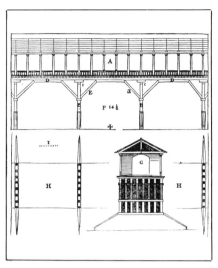

45b Plan, section, elevation (Book II, 1570)

45a Ponte Coperto

113

46. VILLA FORNI - FRACANZAN AND GRENDENE

Montecchio Precalcino (Vicenza)   1560s?

Private and unoccupied. Ask permission of farm administrator to visit.

The attribution of this small villa to Palladio by Muttoni (1740) and Scamozzi (1778) is generally accepted on stylistic grounds. The date of construction is uncertain. The villa was first mentioned in the will of its owner, Girolamo Forni, a dilettante painter and merchant who died in 1610. The sculptural decorations by Alessandro Vittoria, a close friend of Forni, were probably executed in 1576 or 1577, while the sculptor was living in Vicenza.[1]

It is difficult to reconstruct the original site conditions. The *barchessa* to the right, with traces of sixteenth-century frescoes, predates the residential block, while the wall to the left is more recent.

The Villa Forni is Palladio's smallest villa. It is raised on a high service base and commands the site through its elegance and simplicity. Most historians date the building in the early 1540s, before Palladio's first trip to Rome. They cite incongruities between the sculptural decoration and the architecture as evidence that Forni bought the villa from an

46a Villa Forni

unknown original owner and added the sculpture. (Forni was born in about 1530 and could not have commissioned the building at this early date.) However, there is no evidence that the facade has been altered to accept the sculptural decoration. Moreover, in its control of the site as well as its three-dimensional resolution, the villa displays a sophistication characteristic of Palladio's later buildings.

Several aspects of this villa depend on themes formulated at the Villa Poiana: the combination of a Serlian motif with a triangular pediment to mark the entry, the assimilation of the open *serliana* within the architecture of the wall, and the strong coherence between the front and garden elevations. (A balcony has been added to the Serlian window on the garden side.) These themes are adapted to the modest scale of the building, yet at the same time they elevate its significance in a manner appropriate to the needs of an artist-patron; this supports the proposition that Forni commissioned the villa, with a construction date in the 1560s.

[1]Of the original facade reliefs visible in an engraving by Marco Moro, the winged victories in the tympanum and two of the four seasons from the sides of the entry loggia have been removed. Only the Medusa's head on the keystone survives; the other reliefs are reproductions.

46c Engraving (M. Moro)

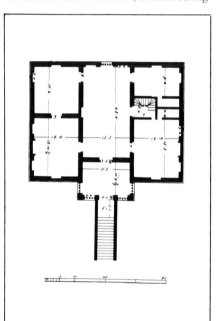

46b Plan (Scamozzi, 1796)

47. PALAZZO BARBARANO - DA PORTO
Contrada Porti, 11, Vicenza
Book II, plates 15, 16   1570–75

Little is known of the circumstances surrounding Palladio's commission to design a palace for Montano Barbaran, except that Barbaran's fortune was consumed by its construction. In March 1570 he sought permission to close a small street between Via di Riale and Via di S. Giacomo, and work on the building fabric probably began immediately. Later in the same year, with construction well advanced, the patron acquired additional property, and Palladio altered his design. The changes are reflected in the two versions illustrated in the *Quattro Libri* (delivered to the printer in November 1570) and in the physical evidence of the palace itself.

Preliminary plan studies (RIBA XVI, 14) indicate Palladio's attempts to organize the irregular site around a central entry hall. One of these conforms to the plan illustrated in the *Quattro Libri*, on which construction began in 1570. The corresponding facade, with a giant order similar to the Palazzo Valmarana, was never realized. Palladio comments on the asymmetry of his published plan and adds that the patron purchased adjoining land so that the palace could be made symmetrical.[1] Late in 1570 Palladio hastily prepared a plate depicting a portion of the revised facade for his publication, indicating his satisfaction with its final resolution.

The palace was brought to its present

47a Palazzo Barbarano

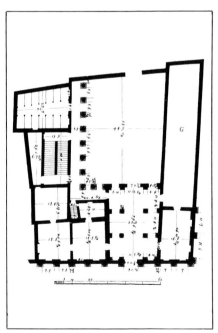

47b Plan (Scamozzi, 1761)

form between 1570 and 1575, with two bays added to the left of its otherwise symmetrical facade, in accordance with the site revisions. The atrium and major rooms to either side correspond to the published plan, while the facade, the rooms in the left side of the plan (including the major stair), and the partially completed courtyard pertain to the revised design.

The facade is distinguished by a strong contrast between the vertical, su-

47c Atrium

47d Courtyard

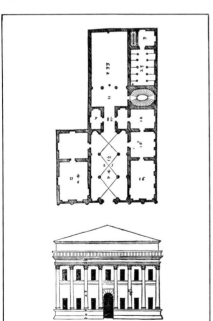

47e Plan, proposed elevation (Book II, 1570)

47f Elevation detail (Book II, 1570)

perimposed orders and the horizontal projection of the corresponding cornices. At the corner, the cornices and columns are terminated separately on each face, reinforcing the independent layering of the adjoining surfaces. On the palace interior the four-columned atrium is combined with a Serlian motif. Only one side of the courtyard colonnade was realized, and its junction with the atrium is abrupt and unresolved, reflecting the decision to enlarge the courtyard when construction was well advanced.

Despite the lack of unity in the executed fragments of the Palazzo Barbarano, this ambitious building indicates Palladio's ongoing efforts to order the irregular site in response to the changing circumstances of its boundaries.

[1]*Book II*, 42.

47g Facade detail

48. PALAZZO THIENE - BONIN (project)*
Corso Andrea Palladio, 13, Vicenza   1572–77?

The Palazzo Thiene, designed and built by Vincenzo Scamozzi, may have been proposed by Palladio, although the extent of his involvement was limited. The palace was built after 1572 for Francesco Thiene, and construction was well advanced by 1586.

If Palladio did provide design sketches, his ideas were modified in execution. The street and courtyard facades are related to the Palazzo Barbarano, although the nonhierarchical use of orders is not Palladian, and the building lacks the plastic control of his late work. It seems closer in spirit to Scamozzi's masterpiece, the Palazzo Trissino (now Palazzo del Commune, Corso Palladio, 98).

48a Palazzo Thiene

48b Elevation (Scamozzi, 1776)

119

49. ARCO DELLE SCALETTE*
Viale Risorgimento Nazionale, Vicenza   1575–76?

The Venetian Commander Giacomo Bragadin erected an arch near the Porta di Monte in 1595, which was executed by Francesco Alabanese. It led to the "street of steps," which at the time was the only pilgrimage route to the Sanctuary of the Madonna on Monte Berico. The initiative for the arch probably began in 1574, when funds were sought to improve the pilgrimage route at the same time that it was decided to enlarge the votive church on the hilltop. Since Palladio may have worked on the church, it is assumed by some scholars that he was responsible for the design of the arch, probably undertaken in preparation for the elaborate processions to the sanctuary in August 1576. It is uncertain why construction was delayed until 1595.

The antique theme of a triumphal arch was adopted in a manner reminiscent of the Loggia del Capitaniato end facade, with niches set between the columns. (These were filled in almost immediately.) The use of an antique precedent — in contrast to the portals in Udine and S. Daniele del Friuli — amplifies the processional qualities of the monument, announcing the beginning of the pilgrimage route at the base of the hill.

49a Arco delle Scalette

49b Elevation (Scamozzi, 1796)

50. VALMARANA CHAPEL
CHURCH OF S. CORONA

Contrada S. Corona, Vicenza   1576–80

Visit: Request permission from the church custodian.

50a Valmarana Chapel

Palladio was commissioned to design Antonio Valmarana's tomb for an unspecified location some time before the patron's death in 1576. In 1597 Valmarana's son Leonardo installed a tomb for himself, his parents, and his brothers adjoining the crypt of S. Corona. This tomb is presumed to be the one designed by Palladio. The lack of resolution in the proportions and detailing are apparently the result of its construction after Palladio's death, perhaps by Pietro da Nanto. The design is related to the side chapels in the Redentore, and the altar is reminiscent of antique sarcophagi.

51a Il Redentore

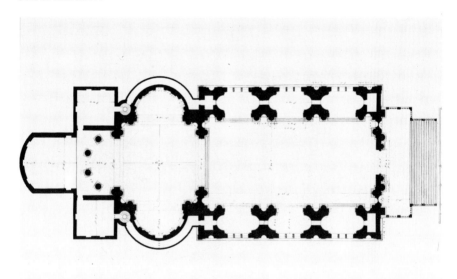

51b Plan (Scamozzi, 1776)

51. IL REDENTORE
Rio della Croce, Venice   1576/7–80

In September 1576, at the height of the plague, the Venetian Senate decided to erect a church to the *Redentore* (Redeemer) and vowed to institute an annual procession to the church to celebrate the anniversary of deliverance. Three sites were proposed to the building committee and designs were drawn in haste for each. In November the committee selected the site controlled by the Capuchins on the Giudecca for its outlying location — often associated with votive churches — as well as for its visibility. Palladio made two proposals for this site, one centralized (favored by Marc'Antonio Barbaro) and the other longitudinal. The latter was chosen in 1577 in keeping with the processional requirements, and additional land was purchased to accommodate the approved scheme. At about the same time, the Capuchin monks ceded more land to provide open space in front of the church for ritual purposes. The first procession was held in July 1577, shortly after the plague ended and two months after construction began.

At the time of Palladio's death the building was in a satisfactory stage, and the church was consecrated in 1592. The sculpture and paintings were not completed until the late seventeenth century, although they are consistent with the original iconographic program.

In response to the complex requirements of the church's votive, processional, and monastic functions, Palla-

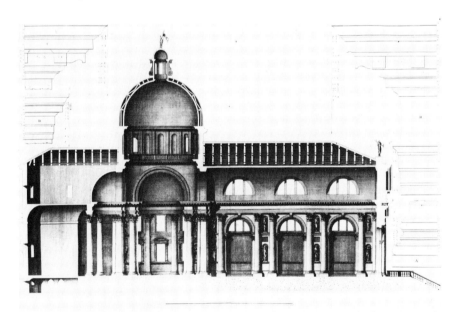

51c Section (Scamozzi, 1776)

dio's design is a brilliant synthesis of diverse architectural themes. There are no direct precedents for the solution. The plan combines three distinct spaces: a longitudinal nave with side chapels (and no aisles), a square presbytery with lateral apses, and a longitudinal choir separated visually by a colonnaded exedra. Each zone is articulated differently: half-columns are used in the nave, pilasters in the lateral apses, and freestanding columns in the terminal apse. Their scenographic juxtaposition provides visual unity, which is reinforced by the uninterrupted cornice.

Palladio assimilated a number of historical motifs within the design. The raised side chapels are separated from the nave by an alternating rhythm derived from the triumphal arch; the barrel-vaulted ceiling is interrupted by thermal windows borrowed from the halls of Roman baths; and the square presbytery capped by a dome is based on the Renaissance tradition of centralized churches. The colonnaded exedra extending into the choir echoes the lateral apses of the presbytery to impart a centralized reading to the longitudinal basilican form.

The facade is a summation of ideas initiated in Palladio's earlier ecclesiastic

51d Elevation (Muttoni, 1740-1748)

buildings for Venice. It is more complex than San Giorgio and more subtle in its impact. To the two intersecting pediments of his earlier designs Palladio added a third pediment in the zone of the paired buttresses, the exterior expression of which anticipates the scenographic layering of the interior. The attic above the central pediment, derived from Palladio's

51e Nave

drawing of the Pantheon (RIBA VIII,9r), contributes to the facade's layered effect. This is also enhanced by the articulation of the orders; their progression from flat to curved and small to large accentuates the rhythmic buildup to the central doorway. The concept for the facade is integrated formally with the interior spatial sequence. Both are tied to the processional experience and its concomitant frontality.

At the annual Feast of the Redeemer, on the third Sunday in July, a temporary bridge over boats lashed together accommodates the procession of worshipers from the Zattere.

52a Le Zitelle

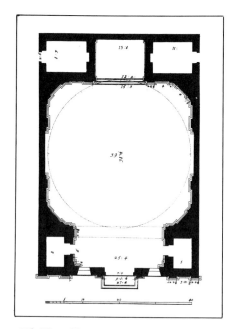

52b Plan (Scamozzi, 1776)

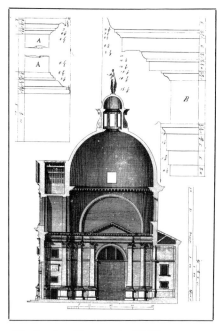

52c Section (Scamozzi, 1776)

52. S. MARIA DELLA PRESENTAZIONE (Le Zitelle)
Guidecca, Venice
1577?–80

An early seventeenth-century source identifies Palladio as the architect of the Church of Le Zitelle (Maidens), part of a religious institute established by a Jesuit prelate, Benedetto Palmi, to assist impoverished young girls. The attribution is justified stylistically, although there are no contemporary documents linking Palladio to the project. He may have been responsible for planning the entire complex of buildings, since the church and adjoining symmetrical wings appear to have been considered as a compositional whole.

52d View of facade

In 1561 Palmi purchased the site facing the Giudecca Canal. The project was delayed by financial difficulties, and Palladio was probably not consulted until sufficient funds were raised to proceed. Construction began in about 1580, the year Palladio died, and the church was essentially completed by 1586.

The imposing character of the facade is consistent with San Giorgio and the Redentore, although at Le Zitelle the formal themes are different. The plan is a perfect square. As in his other centralized churches, Palladio explored distinct architectural motifs, such as the thermal window and paired towers.[1] The twin towers of Le Zitelle, compressed between the facade and the dome, anticipate the Tempietto at Maser.

The church of Le Zitelle lacks the assured proportional control of Palladio's mature work. This may result from his inability to supervise construction or from liberties taken in the building's realization.

[1]Palladio first used these motifs in his 1564 project for the Venetian Church of S. Lucia; however, his design may have been modified in construction, long after his death. S. Lucia was razed in the nineteenth century to make way for the railroad station.

53. S. MARIA NOVA*
Contrada S. Maria Nova, Vicenza 1578

Palladio is occasionally proposed as the architect of S. Maria Nova. The building was sponsored by Ludovico Trento, whose will of 1578 provided for its construction, undertaken between 1585 and 1594. The attribution is credible on stylistic grounds, although the design falters in execution.

S. Maria Nova was intended as an oratory attached to an Augustine convent.

The facade incorporates a triumphal arch motif in a manner reminiscent of the Redentore nave, while the giant order of the large Corinthian hall recalls Palladio's late proposal for the Palazzo da Porto courtyard. The disturbing character of the interior is the result of poor execution and the decorative impulses of later hands.

53a S. Maria Nova

53b Elevation (Scamozzi, 1776)

53c Interior

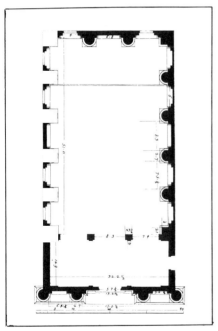

53d Plan (Scamozzi, 1776)

54. PORTA GEMONA
San Daniele del Friuli (Udine)   1579

In 1579 Palladio was asked by the Commune of San Daniele del Friuli to design a
new city gate. Several early designs were
rejected by Cardinal Giovanni Grimani,
Patriarch of Aquileia, who was responsible for carrying out the project.[1] The
executed design is a variation on Palladio's arch in Udine, with changes in proportions and decorative treatment. The
gate was built without Palladio's supervision.

[1]Grimani was also instrumental in Palladio's commission for the facade of San Francesco della Vigna
in Venice.

54a Porta Gemona

55. TEMPIETTO BARBARO
Maser (Treviso) 1579–80

Visit: The interior can be seen by request on Tuesday afternoons when the villa is open.
(See Villa Barbaro.)

An inscription engraved on the frieze of the Barbaro family chapel at Maser names Palladio as architect, Marc'Antonio Barbaro as patron, and 1580 as the date of completion.[1] Palladio's involvement with the villa ended by 1558, yet his association with Marc'Antonio Barbaro extended into the 1560s and 1570s, when Barbaro was instrumental in promoting the architect's Venetian commissions. Palladio may have been at Maser working on this chapel when he died. The decorations were completed to Palladio's design after his death.

The original conditions of the site have not been determined, although the road bisecting the property and leading to the chapel is not original. The peripheral location of the Tempietto with respect to the earlier construction may be due to the uncompromising nature of Palladio's original site plan; no element could be added without disturbing the overall symmetry. This location is both pragmatic and symbolic, for the chapel was to serve as a parish church as well as a family memorial.

This was the first religious structure attached to a Palladian villa, although the custom of including a private chapel in a villa complex was common by the fifteenth century. Formal parallels with the Pantheon give the Tempietto the authority of an antique precedent. Like the Pan-

55a Tempietto Barbaro

theon, the Tempietto combines a cylindrical base with a semicircular dome and no intermediary drum; differences in the proportions and surface treatment make it clear that the Pantheon was an inspiration and not a model for the design.

The idealism associated with centralized plans was religious and philosophical in nature — an intellectual idealism. While Palladio clearly preferred the round form, he used it only when it was appropriate to the architectural program, as with this family memorial. It may also reflect the interests of Marc' Antonio Barbaro, who favored Palladio's centralized scheme for the Redentore.

Barbaro's participation has been cited as the reason for the lack of formal coherence among the elements, although the design is consistent with Palladio's experimental attitude in his last years of practice. His work was never directed toward the attainment of a formal ideal; rather, Palladio's critical attitude toward the language of architecture meant that his search remained open-ended.

[1]Marc'Antonio's brother, Daniele Barbaro, with whom he had commissioned the Villa Barbaro, died in 1570.

55b Villa Barbaro, aerial view

55c View from rear

55d Plan (Scamozzi, 1776)

55e Interior

56. PALAZZO PORTO - BREGANZE
Piazza Castello, Vicenza 1570s

Little is known of the circumstances surrounding this imposing palace fragment facing Piazza Castello, except that it was built sometime after 1571. Vincenzo Scamozzi (1615) refers to it as a work by another architect that was finished to his own design for Count Alessandro Porto, although the date and extent of Scamozzi's involvement are unknown. A seventeenth-century account relates that construction was halted by the author's death (which could refer either to the patron or the architect). In the eighteenth century both Muttoni and Bertotti Scamozzi attributed the incomplete building to Palladio; stylistic evidence supports this claim.

Even in its fragmentary state the facade dominates the large piazza through the power of its giant order. Palladio reinforced the impact of its scale by the plastic treatment of the elements and the resulting effect of *chiaroscuro*. The attic and ground floor are absorbed into the domain of the giant order by a correspondence between the projecting entablature and the podiums on which the columns rest — extending an idea initially explored at the Loggia del Capitaniato.

Muttoni's reconstruction of the plan indicates seven bays with entry through a narrow central passage to a rectangular courtyard. O. B. Scamozzi's plan corresponds more precisely to the built fragment: the courtyard exedra is a logical projection of the existing column fragments. The theatricality of this gesture, with ties to the Villa Serego and Teatro Olimpico, gives credence to Palladio's

authorship of the courtyard as well as the facade.

56a Palazzo Porto

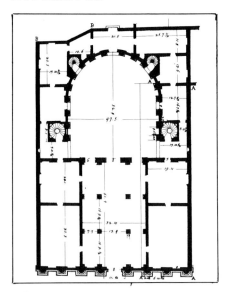

56b Plan (Scamozzi, 1776)

134

57. VILLA PIOVENE*
Lonedo di Lugo (Vicenza)

1570s?

Visit: Grounds only, daily 9–12 and 2–6.

Rivalry between two neighboring families may have motivated the development of the Villa Piovene at the crown of the hill above the Villa Godi, Palladio's first documented building. The major axes of these villas are roughly perpendicular. The Villa Piovene is not in the *Quattro Libri;* it was first attributed to Palladio by Bertotti Scamozzi (1778). The formal evidence is unconvincing; in addition, the uncertainty surrounding the circumstances of the commission and its complicated construction history make it difficult to verify the attribution.

By 1541 the villa owned by Tomasso Piovene consisted of the central portion of the present residential block, with courtyards and outbuildings. By 1575 con-

struction was under way to enlarge the villa by adding four side rooms; this work was interrupted by the patron's death in 1578. The projecting entry portico completed in 1589 was probably not designed by Palladio, for, by the time he died in 1580, his use of this motif was often imitated. Muttoni was responsible for the lateral colonnades, entry gate, and garden stairs added in 1740. Antonio Piovene developed the romantic park during the early nineteenth century.

The central block is similar to the Villa Godi in its general massing and fenestration, yet the Villa Piovene does not display the intelligent rethinking of ideas explored in the earlier building; it merely duplicates a common vernacular

57a Villa Piovene

form. The plan lacks Palladio's subtle hierarchy and seems instead to reflect an imitative and unimaginative treatment of the problem. The site attitude is similarly uninspired.

Scholars have differing opinions concerning Palladio's possible role in this undertaking. Some ascribe the early building to his hand, while others attribute to him the additions of the 1570s (although by that time he was absorbed in numerous Venetian projects and was no longer involved in minor private commissions). At the moment there is no convincing evidence of Palladio's participation in either stage of the villa's development, although further evidence may prove otherwise.

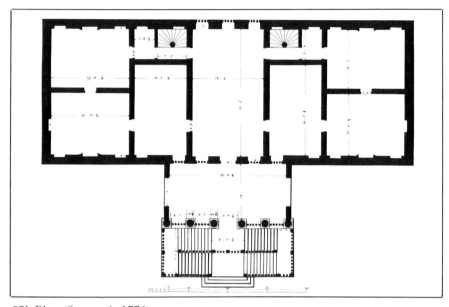

57b Plan (Scamozzi, 1776)

58. TEATRO OLIMPICO
Piazza Matteotti, Vicenza 1580

Visit: 16 March to 15 October: Daily (except Sunday afternoon) 9:30–12:20 and 3–5:30; (16 October to 15 March: 9:30–12:20 and 2–4:30). For group visits, telephone in advance. Tel. 0444/323781.

A group of Vicentine nobles and intellectuals founded the Olympic Academy in 1556. Palladio and his son Silla were included among the members, who held public ceremonies to celebrate the dignified status of the city and their power within it. Such productions traditionally involved elaborate, temporary stage sets, while simple, private performances were frequently produced without sets.

On 15 February 1580 the Academy decided to build a permanent theater, and by the end of the same month the site (in part of the old prisons near the Ponte degli Angeli) had been approved by the City Council and construction begun. Judging from the speed with which it was carried out, Palladio must have started his design for the Teatro Olimpico from the moment the project was conceived. His death on 19 August 1580, while the outer walls were being erected, did not interrupt construction, and the theater was essentially completed three years later.

The Teatro Olimpico is significant in the history of theater design, for it was the first indoor theater to revive the antique tradition of providing a permanent stage and seating. The narrow and irregularly shaped site caused the design to be di-

58a Teatro Olimpico

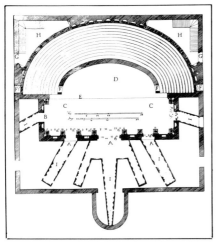

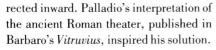

58b Plan (Scamozzi, 1761)

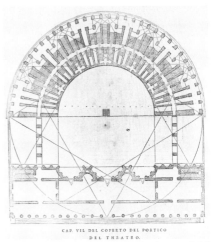

58c Theater of the Ancients (Barbaro, 1556)

rected inward. Palladio's interpretation of the ancient Roman theater, published in Barbaro's *Vitruvius*, inspired his solution.

Palladio created three spatial zones, thematically distinct yet united by their juxtaposition. The first, the *cavea* or audience hall, has an elliptical plan, departing from the semicircular form of the prototype in response to the restricted conditions of the site. The second, the *scenae frons* or stage, is based on the triumphal arch, a motif employed frequently in sixteenth-century dramatic presentations. This was to form a screen to the third zone, a set of flats painted illusionistically, which was to fill the blank openings of the *cavea* wall. It is likely that Palladio intended the perspectives depicted on these flats to converge to a single vanishing point, as indicated in his illustratation of the Theater of the Ancients.

In 1580 it was decided that each member of the Academy should have his likeness produced in plaster to adorn the niches of the *scenae frons*. These figures were carried out from 1584 by a large team of sculptors, including Agostino Rubini, Ruggero Bascape, and Domenico

Fontana. The sculptural decorations reinforce the building's symbolic role by glorifying the power of the aristocracy and celebrating the Academy's presence in the cultural life of the city.

In 1584 Palladio's design was altered by the addition of perspective sets beyond the *cavea* wall, on a plot of adjoining property purchased in 1580 after Palladio's death. They were designed by Vincenzo Scamozzi for a production of *Oedipus Rex* and remained as permanent fixtures, irrevocably modifying Palladio's architectural intentions. In addition Scamozzi enlarged the side doors of the *scenae frons* to increase the sets' visibility, extended the walls at the edge of the stage, and hung a curtain from festoons added to the ceiling. There is no indication of Palladio's proposals for the ceilings; the painted sky over the *cavea* was a later modification. The vestibule, built in 1584, was beyond the limits of his responsibility.

Scamozzi's introduction of perspective sets contributes to misperceptions about the relationship of this building to Palladio's work as a whole. Scamozzi's false perspectives have diverging vanish-

58d Scenae frons

ing points. Moreover, by rendering the spatial illusion three-dimensionally, Scamozzi severed the connection between the perspective portion of the set and the overall architectural idea.

Rather than use painterly principles to distinguish the space of the action from that of the audience in the manner favored by Scamozzi and Serlio, Palladio relied solely on architectural means. He created three distinct zones, using architectural discontinuity to reinforce visual unity. The junction between the audience hall and the stage is marked by changes in architectural vocabulary alone. Discontinuity is extended to the stage itself, where the rationally constructed space in front of the *cavea* wall was to be distinguished from the illusionistic space beyond implied by the perspective flats. (By his intended use of perspective Palladio indicated that it is a system based on

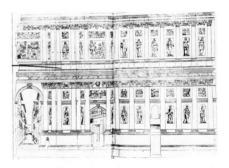

58e Theater of the Ancients (Barbaro, 1556)

illusion rather than a representation of reality.) The three zones are radically different yet united through their juxtaposition. Scenographic means control the entire solution, not merely the space of the stage; this idea permeated Palladio's architectural vision.

139

ILLUSTRATIONS

The British Architectural Library, RIBA, London: 10, 13, 15, 19, 22, 33, 34, 35, 2c, 2f, 3b, 4b, 6e, 6f, 11c, 12d, 14a, 15b, 23c, 24c, 25b, 38c.

Centro di Studi di Architettura "Andrea Palladio," Vicenza: 1, 2, 3, 4, 5, 6, ?, 16, 17, 18, 20, 24, 26, 29, 32, 39, 44, 45, 46, 47, 1a, 1c, 2a, 2b, 2d, 2e, 3 ., 5a, 5b, 5c, 6a, 6c, 6d, 9a, 9c, 7a, 7c, 7d, 8a, 8c, 9a, 9c, 10a, 11a, 12a, 12b, 13a, 14b, 15a, 15c, 15d, 15e, 15f, 16a, 16c, 18a, 18b, 18d, 18e, 19a, 19c, 19d, 19e, 20a, 20c, 20d, 20e, 21a, 21c, 21d, 22a, 22e, 22g, 23a, 27a, 27c, 27d, 30a, 30c, 32a, 32c, 33b, 34a, 34c, 34d, 34e, 34f, 35a, 36a, 36d, 38a, 39b, 41a, 41b, 41c, 41d, 41e, 41f, 41g, 43c, 44a, 44b, 44c, 44d, 44e, 46a, 46c, 47a, 47b, 47c, 47d, 48b, 50a, 51a, 51b, 51c, 51d, 51e, 53c, 55a, 55b, 55c, 55d, 55e, 56a, 56b, 57a, 57b, 58a, 58b, 58c, 58d, 58e.

Museo Civico, Vicenza: 9, 27, 28.

Professor Dr. Bernhard Rupprecht, Erlangen: 31, 22b.

Rudolf Wittkower, *Architectural Principles in the Age of Humanism* (London: Tiranti, 1962): 7.

SELECTED BIBLIOGRAPHY

Ackerman, James S.
Palladio. Harmondsworth: Penguin, 1966.
Palladio's Villas. Locust Valley, NY: J. J. Augustine, 1967.

Argan, Giulio Carlo.
"The Importance of Sammicheli in the Formation of Palladio," in *Renaissance Art*, ed. by C. Gilbert. New York: Harper & Row, 1970.

Burns, Howard.
Andrea Palladio, 1508–1580: The portico and the farmyard. London: Arts Council of Great Britain, 1975.

Cevese, Renato.
Le Ville della provincia di Vicenza, 2 vols. Milan: Rusconi, 1971.

Lewis, Douglas.
The Drawings of Andrea Palladio. Baltimore: International Exhibitions Foundation, 1981.

Palladio, Andrea.
The Four Books on Architecture, trans. by Isaac Ware, 1738. New York: Dover, 1965.

Puppi, Lionello.
Andrea Palladio. Boston: New York Graphics Society, 1975.

Wittkower, Rudolf.
Architectural Principles in the Age of Humanism. London: Alec Tiranti, 1962.
Palladio and English Palladianism. New York: Thames & Hudson, 1974.

Zorzi, Gian Giorgio.
Le Chiese e i ponti di Andrea Palladio. Venice: Neri Pozza, 1966.
Le Opere Pubbliche e i palazzi privati di Andrea Palladio. Venice: Neri Pozza, 1965.
Le Ville e i Teatri di Andrea Palladio. Venice: Neri Pozza, 1968.

Bollettino del Centro Internazionale di Studi di Architettura "Andrea Palladio," Vicenza, from 1960.

VENETO

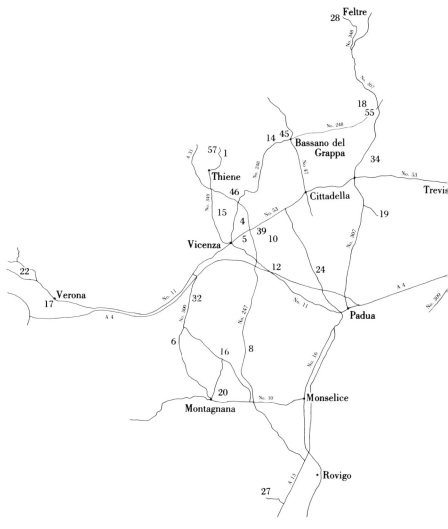

1 Villa Godi, Lonedo
4 Villa Valmarana, Vigardolo
5 Villa Gazzotti, Bertesina
6 Villa Pisani, Bagnolo
8 Villa Saraceno, Finale
10 Villa Thiene, Quinto Vicentino
12 Villa Chiericati, Vancimuglio
14 Villa Angarano, Angarano

15 Villa Caldogno, Caldogno
16 Villa Poiana, Poiana
17 Palazzo della Torre, Verona
18 Villa Barbaro, Maser
19 Villa Cornaro, Piombino Dese
20 Villa Pisani, Montagnana
21 Palazzo Antonini, Udine
22 Villa Serego, Santa Sophia

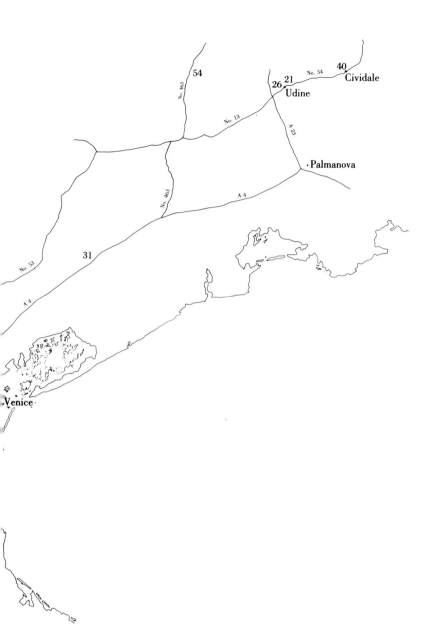

VICENZA

VENICE

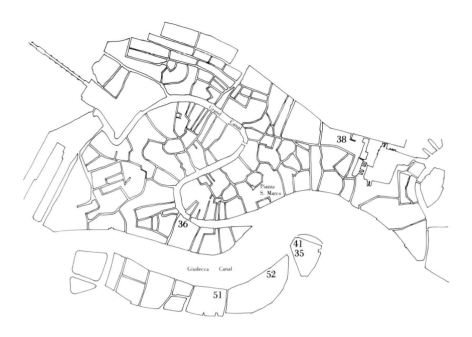

35 S. Giorgio Maggiore, Refectory
36 Monastery of the Carita (Accademia)
38 S. Francesco della Vigna
41 S. Giorgio Maggiore
51 Il Redentore
52 S. Maria della Presentazione (Le Zitelle)

INDEX

Locations